A CASE FOR KINDNESS
A New Look at the Teaching Ethic

"The right book at the right time. Broidy offers readers a scholarly examination of kindness, both sociologically and educationally. In our current era of increasing tribalism and unkindness – exhibited daily on the evening news, Broidy offers a path forward toward more healthy classrooms and a more deliberative society by mapping a direct link between kindness, immediacy and democracy."

—PHIL KELLY, PH.D., PROFESSOR
CURRICULUM, INSTRUCTION, & FOUNDATIONAL STUDIES
BOISE STATE UNIVERSITY

"All educators are familiar with the power of kindness in the teaching-learning process. So much of our success depends on the quality of the student-teacher relationship. Classrooms and schools like personal relationships have marked boundaries and our ability to transcend those boundaries is greatly enhanced by kindness. This book helps makes the argument of why this is so and why our attention to kindness goes to the heart of moral education. Diverting our attention from this topic lessens what it means to be human and humane."

—PAUL WANGEMANN, PH.D., ASSOCIATE PROFESSOR
DAVID O. MCKAY SCHOOL OF EDUCATION
BRIGHAM YOUNG UNIVERSITY

"Steve Broidy's *A Case For Kindness* is a convincing call for the development and cultivation of kindness in the classroom. He provides careful contextualization and clear definition of just what kindness is and how it should form a teaching ethic. All sorts of teachers can benefit from reading and considering Broidy's much-needed and thoughtful book."

—CHRISTOPHER BECKHAM, PH.D., INSTRUCTOR,
FOUNDATIONAL AND GRADUATE STUDIES IN EDUCATION
MOREHEAD STATE UNIVERSITY

THE ACADEMY BOOK SERIES IN EDUCATION

Steven P. Jones and Eric C. Sheffield, *Editors*

The *Academy Book Series in Education* focuses serious attention on the often-missed nexus of educational theory and educational practice. The volumes in this series, both monographs and edited collections, consider theoretical, philosophical, historical, sociological, and other conceptual orientations in light of what those orientations can tell readers about successful classroom practice and sound educational policy. In this regard, the *Academy Series* aims to offer a wide array of themes including school reform, content specific practice, contemporary problems in higher education, the impact of technology on teaching and learning, matters of diversity, and other essential contemporary issues in educational thought and practice.

BOOKS IN THE SERIES

Why Kids Love (and Hate) School: Reflections on Difference
Why Kids Love (and Hate) School: Reflections on Practice
Making Sense of Race in Education: Practices for Change in Difficult Times
A Case for Kindness: A New Look at the Teaching Ethic

Steven P. Jones is a professor in the College of Education at Missouri State University and Executive Director of the Academy for Educational Studies. He is author of *Blame Teachers: The Emotional Reasons for Educational Reform*—a book that investigates how and why so many people try to justify educational change by deriding the efforts and effectiveness of our public school teachers. A former high school English teacher in Jefferson County, Colorado, Jones received his B.A. in English from the University of Denver, his M.A. in Educational Administration from the University of Colorado (Boulder), and his Ph.D. in Curriculum and Instruction from the University of Chicago.

Eric C. Sheffield is Professor and Department Chair of Educational Studies at Western Illinois University in Macomb. He is also founding editor of the Academy for Educational Studies' peer reviewed journal, *Critical Questions in Education*. A former English teacher in Putman County Florida, Sheffield received his B.A. in Philosophy from Illinois College, and his M.Ed (English Education) & Ph.D (Philosophy of Education) from the University of Florida.

The editors of the *Academy Book Series in Education* are interested in reviewing manuscripts and proposals for possible publication in the series. Scholars who wish to be considered should email their proposals, along with two sample chapters and current CVs, to the editors. For instructions and advice on preparing a prospectus, please refer to the Myers Education Press website at http://myersedpress.com/sites/stylus/MEP/Docs/Prospectus%20Guidelines%20MEP.pdf. You can send your material to:

Steven P. Jones
Eric C. Sheffield
academyedbooks@gmail.com

A CASE
FOR KINDNESS

A CASE
FOR KINDNESS

A New Look at the Teaching Ethic

By Steve Broidy

Myers
Education
Press

GORHAM, MAINE

Myers
Education
Press

Copyright © 2019 | Myers Education Press, LLC

Published by Myers Education Press, LLC
P.O. Box 424 Gorham, ME 04038

Myers Education Press is an academic publisher specializing in books, e-books, and digital content in the field of education. All of our books are subjected to a rigorous peer-review process and produced in compliance with the standards of the Council on Library and Information Resources.

Library of Congress Cataloging-in-Publication Data available from Library of Congress.

13-digit ISBN 978-1-9755-0201-0 (paperback)
13-digit ISBN 978-1-9755-0200-3 (hard cover)
13-digit ISBN 978-1-9755-0202-7 (library networkable e-edition)
13-digit ISBN 978-1-9755-0203-4 (consumer e-edition)

Printed in the United States of America.

All first editions printed on acid-free paper that meets the American National Standards Institute Z39-48 standard.

Books published by Myers Education Press may be purchased at special quantity discount rates for groups, workshops, training organizations, and classroom usage. Please call our customer service department at 1-800-232-0223 for details.

Cover design by Sophie Appel

Visit us on the web at www.myersedpress.com to browse our complete list of titles.

TABLE OF CONTENTS

PREFACE

THIS BOOK IS THE product of at least a quarter century of papers I have developed on the subject of kindness. The arguments and observations of many of these papers have found a place in this volume. I confess that I am surprised that the effort of so much thought has produced, in the end, so brief a volume. I only hope that the reader will find at least some value in so little a work.

I want to thank Drs. Steven Jones and Eric Sheffield for their valuable advice and their, yes, kind encouragement during the development of this book.

IN THIS BOOK, I argue that educators would do well to carefully consider the kind of relationship they seek to develop and maintain with their students. Both common teaching wisdom and a substantial body of research point to that relationship as one of the key determiners of student engagement, student learning, and student personal growth. One recent study (Jackson, 2018), for example, found that a relationship with students that impacts students' non-cognitive skills, such as adaptability, motivation, and self-restraint, is ten times more predictive of students' long-term success than teachers' impact on test scores.

The particular sort of relationship I will argue for, one based in teachers' development and exercise of ethical sensibility that gives precedence to kindness, requires considerable clarification, explanation, and support. While the "care ethic" that Nel Noddings (1984, 2005) and others have argued for is well known, my argument is not theirs, though there is much value in this tradition; in fact, I will take issue with a number of features of the arguments supporting that view. Moreover, the very notion of an "ethical sensibility," a concept I will argue is central both logically and practically to our relationship with others, represents a departure from current discussions of the teacher-student relationship.

I hope that, by the close of this book, the reader will recognize in my argument a starting place for both the formation of educational policy and professional relationships affecting our most important clients, our students.

The Teaching Ethic and Teaching Relationships

I like to begin an introductory Teacher Education course by asking students to complete this sentence stem: "As a professional educator, I'll teach. . . ." Students' answers tell me much about their preconceptions concerning the nature of teaching and the work they'll do. Most often, students will complete the sentence by mentioning the subjects they intend to teach ("I'll teach English, history, etc."). Sometimes they mention the level of schooling at which they anticipate teaching: "I'll teach fifth grade" (or high school, etc.).

There are other sorts of answers that pop up occasionally: location (inner city, rural schools) or job or vocation ("I'll teach for a living").

We can infer from this variety of responses that many prospective teachers envision the central point of their work and professional lives as, variously, their subject areas, the level of schooling with which they'll identify, the sorts of communities in which they'll work, their ability to navigate their workplaces, or the importance of what they will do. Whatever their answers, however, they are always simple in structure, with one direct object.

After I have looked at and analyzed student responses for a given course, I go back to that teaching sentence with students; I fill it out in its actual complexity, reflected by multiple direct and indirect objects and many attendant clauses. While this exercise calls their attention to the many things they must learn about, attend to, and master as prospective teachers, they seem to be most taken aback by something else for which I argue. I tell them that to reflect what is most important for student engagement and success in school they should begin the teaching sentence this way: "I'll teach *each student and group of students. . . .*"

What this grammatical activity is meant to introduce is the importance of teachers' relationships with their students, both individuals and groups. This is in contrast to the ways that the tasks of teaching are generally and publicly discussed, primarily in terms of raising test scores. The tangible "rewards of teaching," such as they are, seem primarily to be determined by students' acquisition of a rather limited knowledge set, as measured on standardized tests. But classroom life begins and ends with the relationships between and among students and teachers. That is what both sets of people live with, for during students' school years a very large portion of their respective waking lives—more than 13%—is in instruction by age 18, with nearly that much in school activities outside of instruction as well. In many ways, it is that relationship that helps determine students' academic success. Learning, of many kinds, is the goal, but relationship is the medium in which learning grows.

Moreover, it is the relationship between teacher and student(s) that is the central benefit of face-to-face learning. In a period of American education that increasingly centralizes control of learning at a distance from the classroom, finds online instruction increasingly attractive, standardizes curriculum, and narrowly defines academic success, how do *teachers* make a difference for the better in students' lives and learning? I argue that it is through teachers' relationships with their students that this may be accomplished.

It is partly because teachers' professional lives are so bound up with the "relationship loads" they carry that teaching is essentially a moral activity. A successful teacher-student relationship is not only a matter of what teacher acts are likely to directly result in student learning as much of the process-product research tradition of the late 20th and early 21st century might lead one to believe. A successful teacher-student relationship, like a successful parent-child relationship, depends in large measure on teachers' consideration for the general and academic welfare of their students and for acting, in the context of their professional commitments to and aspirations for their students, in ways that seek to avoid harm and promote well-being in the short and long terms. These considerations and actions are part of what I will call a "teaching ethic."

What Is a "Teaching Ethic"?

To understand what counts as a teaching ethic, we must examine the ways that teachers decide and act on matters that involve their relationship with their students and their concern for students' welfare and learning. To speak of those decisions as an "ethic" also implies that the process is continuing and customary. A teaching ethic is not the entire range of professional ethics; but a teaching ethic is not just an ethos—a coherent set of values in practice. It is that, but it is also more. It is the playing out of a certain sensibility with regard to teachers' relationships with students and the decisions affecting students in the instructional environment.

The process that describes both singular ethical decisions and the foundation of such decision-making is best described as a "sensibility."

What I mean by a "sensibility" is a *recurrent and coherent set of emotions and feelings, sensitivities/perceptions, dispositions, and conscious priorities that tend to both directly influence choice and provide a privileged set of premises in reflective decision-making.* In chapter three, I will explain the role that teachers' ethical sensibility plays in the ethical judgments they make and the relationships they form with their students.

Why Kindness?

As I write this, there is no shortage of interest in kindness. A plethora of organizations and websites tout the value of kindness in purportedly making the world a better place and the givers and receivers of kindness happier and more satisfied with their lives. After generations of relegation to a position as an ethical sidelight, kindness is "hot."

The case for kindness I will make in this book begins by noting the ill-defined nature of our talk about kindness and the need for clarity before any useful argument for its value in a teaching ethic can occur. The groups promoting kindness today almost uniformly ignore that unclarity, so their programs are made confusing and their arguments are riddled with ambiguities and equivocations. The role of the first two chapters is to point out and deal with that unclarity, resulting in a detailed analysis of the concept of kindness. The reader will discover that kindness is a complex concept and a complex activity. Moreover, kindness as the central feature of an ethical sensibility, I will argue in chapters four and five, is the foundation of a teaching ethic that will best serve the teacher-student relationship, helping it to address student welfare and success.

Chapter four also contains suggestions to educators on how to develop a kindness-oriented teaching ethic. There are many approaches that will address this process, and some of these are already available to teacher-educators and teacher-coaches.

Chapter five extends the argument for kindness in the teaching ethic to long-term ideal aims for educating. The case for kindness includes its value in achieving a coherent vision of what, in the end, we might educate for. This consideration of ultimate purposes of educating is one that educators and policymakers have, for some time, overlooked or taken for granted but may well be a key to making the decisions and direction of education more valuable to educators, students, their parents, and the general public.

CHAPTER ONE

EDUCATION, ETHICS, AND KINDNESS

THIS IS A BOOK about the teaching ethic, and about kindness, an ill-defined and therefore often equivocated quality of our actions and our character. Trivialized as supererogatory by many moral philosophers, made homely by a tradition of children's literature, and conflated with or absorbed into dozens of concepts that are near relatives, the power and value of kindness as a separate notion has often been misconstrued. Nominally popularized today as a kind of easy, moral cure-all, kindness is nevertheless a sort of moral stepchild in Western culture, especially American culture. It is a quality of which we say we are very fond but which we employ in argument and policy very uncertainly.

I hope in this book to lay out an argument for the value to teachers and students of an ethical sensibility of kindness as the basis of a preferable teaching ethic. But if the reader is to be convinced that a teaching ethic that has as its central feature an emphasis on kindness that educators should strive to develop and maintain, conceptual clarity is a prerequisite. This chapter begins that task by noting the quality of Americans' interest in kindness and their confusion about the nature of the object of that interest.

Benevolence, Beneficence, and Kindness

A whole host of moral concepts, many of which I will later attempt to clarify and distinguish from kindness, have in common a connection to, and in some ways may be subsumed under, the broad notion of "benevolence." Benevolence is an attitudinal and affective term; that is, when we recognize benevolence, part of what we recognize is someone's intention and desire to bring about a better state in another. This is accompanied by recognizing in one who acts benevolently a response of pleasure to another's improved state or distress at a worsening state.

These features of benevolence imply a degree of both empathy and sympathy. That is, one's attitude would not be benevolent but merely benign if it did not include some level of awareness of the other's actual state and some level of commitment to at least a generalized plan for bettering the other's state. However, benevolence may be more or less informed concerning the other's state and what would better it. For example, I may still be acting with benevolence if, wishing to help, I cover with a blanket an unconscious person on a cold street corner and then walk on—oblivious to the fact that the person I've covered is seriously ill and needs immediate medical aid.

Benevolence may motivate certain acts; it isn't identifiable through the act per se. For instance, if I give a warm coat to a shivering child because I want to relieve her discomfort, then I am acting benevolently. But if, instead, I give her the coat only because I will be fired from my teaching position if I do not, then my act is arguably not a benevolent one, even if the child is grateful to receive the coat and the child's condition is improved through receiving the coat. Perhaps more controversially, the same act would arguably also not be a benevolent one if its motivation were *solely* to comply with some religious, social, or cultural requirement to "clothe the naked." *Mere* obedience to convention or rule disqualifies an action as a product of benevolence.

Despite this language, which refers to "acting benevolently," benevolence is a term that picks out intentions rather than effects. That is, intent and desire to help do not, alone, make for a beneficent act—one that actually helps. Even acts that have disastrous results, that do harm or allow harm to come to others, may be benevolent; and many acts that actually help may be done without the intent or desire to do so. As an instance of the former, a teacher, whose praise of a student in class results in that student being beaten up after school by a jealous classmate, can be seen to have acted benevolently, given the intention and desire to improve the beaten student's scholastic state. Even acts that have no effects on others at all may be recognizably benevolent. If I were to write, but not send, a note to a student, sincerely wishing that student success, and if such a note reflected my real pleasure in the prospect of the student's happiness with that success, then writing that note would clearly be a benevolent action, even if I never send the note.

Alternatively, a teacher may announce in class the perfect score an unpopular student has achieved on an assignment, intending only to motivate the rest of the class, but with the result that the class now sees the chosen student as one more worthy than before of good treatment. This act isn't done benevolently, yet it can be understood as beneficent (i.e., an act that creates good for another; (Stanford) Encyclopedia of Philosophy, 2013).

Benevolence, in this analysis, seems to be an insufficient basis for building a moral program, but analyzing the concept does make us aware of the fact that the intentional and emotional conditions that pick out benevolence are shared by a range of concepts that have important connections to our moral lives. These include, among many others, compassion, mercy, considerateness, hospitableness, generosity, and kindness. Concerning kindness, we may note that benevolent intention and emotion are what is missing in unkindness, and the opposite of benevolence is necessary to recognizing cruelty.

It is not difficult to see, given the overlap among benevolence concepts, how such concepts can be conflated or confused with one another. Though I will later try to show how much more is required of kindness than intentions and emotions, it is understandable that we often, mistakenly, think of kindness as no more than acts done with benevolence. A cynical saying, alternatively attributed to the mobster Al Capone and the comedian "Professor" Irwin Corey, goes like this: "You can get much further with a kind word and a gun than you can with a kind word alone." The reduction of kindness to intentions and emotions alone is probably what gives such cynics their reservations about kindness as a practical focus for moral activity. It seems likely that such conceptual confusion also plays a role in the trivializing of kindness as a central moral feature.

Origins of Conceptual Confusion About Kindness

The concept of kindness has historically been both ill-defined and controversial. Western religious traditions have seen it as morally important, but Western philosophy, at least after ancient Greece, has seen it as not as important as justice, and on some views nearly incidental to the correct moral life. Some have even argued that if human nature is a naturally selfish one, then kindness is a danger to survival and prosperity.

Phillips and Tyler (2010) point out the following:

1. The origin of the term "kindness" is "kinship"; that is, acting in a way that regards the needs of close family. Thus, this line in *Hamlet* is ambiguous: "I must be cruel to be kind."

2. Greek analogues of "kind" were "philanthropia" (love of humankind), "caritas" (open heartedness), and Stoics' "oykeosis" (attachment to others).

3. Marcus Aurelius said "Kindness is mankind's greatest delight."

4. Hobbes wrote that human existence is a "warre of alle against alle." Some parts of Western philosophical tradition see competitiveness, independence, self-reliance, or self-interest as the basis of moral life. And benevolent feelings and acts are at root self-serving or evidence of weakness.

Western religious thought about kindness occasionally offers strong claims about the importance of kindness in both moral and prudential choices. The Talmud, for instance (Berachot, 17a), makes the claim that "[t]he highest form of wisdom is kindness." This view is echoed by Jean Jacques Rousseau's question in Book II of his *Emile:* "What wisdom can you find that is greater than kindness?" His answer is that kindness is a universal duty toward all who are "not foreign to humanity." The notion of wisdom as central to useful and morally justifiable decision-making has been argued for by researchers such as Robert Sternberg (1998), who finds that wisdom, as distinct from common sense, centers on successful reasoned decisions—which, in turn, also applies to kindness if it is to be a "high" form of wisdom. He argues that children as young as middle school age have it, that it can be fostered, and that if we don't identify it in children before college, it can be "too late." Wisdom, Sternberg (1998) says intriguingly but vaguely, involves balancing the needs of all involved in a situation—a notion I will take up in chapter two as crucial to recognizing kind acts.

But if wisdom is an important goal for our development, and kindness is to some extent a form of wisdom, then it becomes a matter of more than passing interest to exhibit, clarify, and promote kindness in central settings of children's existence such as schooling. Yet kindness is and has been ill-defined. Western culture historically and American culture today have been almost willfully sloppy in offering confusing and conflating accounts of kindness.

Jewish and Christian religious writings, central to Western moral thought, provide one major source of confusion and equivocation. For example, "chesed," the term usually translated as kindness in Jewish liturgy and philosophical texts, is as likely to be translated as "mercy," a term I will argue is significantly different in meaning and in practical consequence from kindness. In the New Testament, writers such as Paul are notorious for conflating kindness with a large array of similar concepts, to such an extent that it is difficult to see any clear, or at least consistent, differences among kindness, love, charity, meekness, compassion, mercy, and a variety of other similar terms. *The Encyclopedia of Religion and Ethics* matter-of-factly notes that in early Christian writings, kindness means at least the following variety of things: a forgiving disposition, love of enemies, mercy over legality, tenderness to small children, the golden rule, and good works. Here and in most religious uses of kindness, the term seems to be used to mean almost any benevolently intended and/or beneficent action.

Today, kindness talk seems to be everywhere in American culture. But confusion and conflation mark our thinking about kindness, both in ordinary public speech and in the arguments of actual advocates for kindness as a central moral virtue. A typical example of the former, one that calls to mind the pointed ambiguity (referencing both the Prince's unfortunate family tendencies and hoped-for good outcomes) of the line from *Hamlet* that speaks to a need to "be cruel only to be kind," comes from the Partnership for a Drug-Free America in a *New York Times* advertisement on the dangers of drugs. The ad warns, "You could kill an addict with kindness. There's no escape for a drug addict. The spiral goes down. Fast. And the bottom is a nightmare. Even death. An addict's only chance is treatment. But kindness won't help somebody who's hooked. If you have a drug user working for you, you've got to offer the hard choice: Get well or get out. It's not pleasant."

The ad seems to conflate kindness with accommodation in arguing for our approach to those who are addicted: If we "baby them along," the ad argues, we are causing addicts to get worse. This may be true, but in calling such accommodation kindness, the ad may lead us to overlook the possibility that the tough response advocated may, in the long run, be one that we, and presumably the addicts affected by that response, would see as kind. So, is our kindness good or bad for addicts? Equivocation makes answering more difficult than it needs to be.

Organizations have lately arisen devoted to promoting kindness, whether or not they can present a clear account of the term. Groups such as the Random Acts of Kindness Foundation, the Kindness Revolution, the Human Kindness Foundation, SpreadKindness, Random Acts, and others share a stated commitment to helping others and offer numerous examples of what such help might include. But these groups, in their writings, never seem to get around to clarifying kindness in ways that might help their clientele to distinguish one sort of helping act from another, or one preferred motivation for acting from others less to be preferred.

This failure to clarify, except through assorted examples, can lead to practical difficulties. In SpreadKindness's (n.d) set of examples on its website, as of this writing, clients see instances of courtesy (let another driver you meet at a stop sign go first), generosity (give a homeless person the leftovers from your restaurant meal), and general positiveness (write an anonymous, loving note and post it for strangers to find). Yet that sort of courtesy can make its receivers and others around them impatient and frustrated at delays. Leaving notes lying around can be ignored or produce anger at the clutter. And giving leftovers to the homeless can be seen as patronizing and disrespectful rather than as kind. Such examples may leave readers with questions about both the meaning of kindness and about the benefits of purportedly kind acts.

There is another very practical effect of this unclarity: the group Random Acts (n.d) actually offers, at this time, to fund kindness projects, but nowhere in its stated application process does it offer an account of what it understands to be a definition of kindness. This leaves potential applicants to guess whether their proposals meet guidelines or to offer an explicit defense of their projects as being ones that exemplify kindness, without any reason to believe that the organization will find such an argument relevant. The application guidelines merely say that the reviewer will notify the applicant of the final decision—seemingly, an arbitrary process, and an unkind one at that.

Finally, and at the risk of being too cynical about groups whose stated mission is to help and to promote helping, I can't help but point out that what all these organizations have in common, judging from their websites, is a concern to receive donations or sell books—a first opportunity, it would seem, for potential members to engage in a "kind" act.

Kindness and Goodness in American Educational History

In American education, moral instruction has almost always been recognized as an important feature of schooling. And American textbooks have borrowed extensively from the traditional Judeo-Christian confusion and equivocation about kindness, discussed earlier. The benevolence and beneficence language peculiar to 17th- through 19th-century American educational aims for students stressed something called "goodness." The importance of goodness as an objective of school moral education during that period often focused on what texts of the era called "kindness." But the interest in goodness also played a role in obscuring the importance of kindness as a moral value. Throughout the period's school texts, goodness, like today's discussions of kindness, was a complex, shifting, and ambiguous concept.

Some Christian sources see kindness as a trait that desires happiness of others, whereas goodness is doing things that advance others' happiness. But others translate "chrestotes" as the opposite, where goodness is all one's manner of acting and kindness is deeds. Sometimes that term is translated as "good *and* kind" (as in the New International Version Bible, the New Living Translation, and the New American Standard Bible). Education's emphasis on goodness as both a quality of particular acts and as a feature of character served to further confuse educative goals and the role of kindness in such goals.

There is little doubt that American education in the earliest centuries of settlement and nationhood was greatly concerned with what Nel Noddings (1984) has called "the production of a moral citizenry" (pp. 215–216). Ruth Miller Elson (1964), in her insightful analysis of the "hidden curriculum" of common school texts, stated rather categorically that "[t]he purpose of the nineteenth-century American public schools was to train citizens in character and proper principles" (p. 1).

That continuing concern for developing moral citizens reflected the mostly very practical agendas of those who commissioned and produced the school texts and other materials that students encountered. And for American schoolboys and schoolgirls, from colonial days through the early decades of the 20th century, goodness was an important feature of the moral agendas.

[handwritten marginalia: connection; b/t Judeo-Christian confusion + American education]

Textbooks of the 18th through early 20th centuries were the descendants of the early American readers whose origin was in the "primer."
Primers, in turn, were as much directly concerned with imbuing religious
dogma and providing resources for devotion as with providing practice and
rudimentary instruction in reading. The common school textbooks of the
19th century, like the people who created and disseminated them, retained a
conception of morality and good character that looked back to the Puritans,
even as it looked forward to creating a republican triumph and economic
and political expansion. And goodness was evidently seen as a key feature of
the sort of moral character that would contribute to those ends.

The moral tone of these early texts is already evident in an entry from
The Royal Primer, a 1787 reader that Clifton Johnson (1963) called a late
version of *The New England Primer*, the first recognizable "textbook"
available to colonial schoolchildren. In "The Rewards of Virtue" from *The
Royal Primer*, Miss Goodchild, raised to be pious in the early Puritan sense,
is orphaned. But she meets success: a loving, rich husband and friends who
so love her that "they strove to make her happy." All of this is because
of "her undissembled Piety, a decent Modesty, which showed itself in her
Actions, an innocent Simplicity, and a Heart full of Goodness" (p. 27). It
is this goodness, buttressed to no small degree by riches, that later in life
enables her "to gratify the generous Dispositions of her Heart, in relieving
any distrest honest Man; and in promoting the substantial Benefit of all
around her" (p. 90).

Here, "goodness" is a simpler and clearer notion, if already an old-fash-
ioned one. It seems to refer to the benevolent intentions and emotions and
the generous actions of charity. Goodness in this example is closely associated both with tangible personal advancement and with the maintenance of
a lifestyle calculated to help society achieve its most cherished goals. Piety,
in Puritan New England, was not just the outward sign of personal grace,
but the whole community's reason for being, and was a model for the world
to emulate.

The association of goodness with personal advancement, for the purpose
of furthering common goals, became a continuing moral theme in common
school textbooks, especially in the readers. In terms that have clear asso-
ciations with Puritan theology and with John Wesley's observations about
the connections between piety and material success, Ruth Elson (1964)
described the relationship: "God does not entrust wealth to the successful

man for self-indulgence but for the benefit of the community" (p. 217). In strikingly similar language, some modern communitarians, such as Robert Bellah and colleagues (1985), have defined real freedom not as the right to do what one pleases, but as the right to do what's right. This is a view that common school texts would have recognized and approved of.

Goodness became a more complex concept, with more alternative formulations, as the 19th century advanced. Though much the same sense of the concept I described earlier informs the advice in "Family Friendship" from *The Progressive Reader or Juvenile Monitor* in 1837—"If they [brothers or sisters] have any thing which you would like to have, do not be angry with them, or want to get it from them. If you have any thing they like, share it with them" (Atwood, 1830, p. 1)—texts soon began to both intensify the benevolence associated with goodness and to add other features to the concept. In "How to Win a Precious Jewel" from Charles Sanders' *The School Reader* (1846), a rich man will give a precious jewel to the son of his who performs "the most noble and generous action within three months" (pp. 53–54). One son returns to a stranger what the stranger entrusts with him, but father calls this "just." The second son jumps in and saves a drowning child, but the father calls this "the dictate of humanity" (p. 54). The third son finds his mortal enemy asleep on a precipice, unaware of where he is. Risking his own life, the third son pulls the enemy to safety; this the father calls noble and generous, "truly the spirit of the gospel of Christ, who has said, 'Love your enemies, bless them that curse you, and do good to them that hate you'" (p. 54). Goodness, in common school texts, often became entangled with sectarian righteousness.

The growing complexity of goodness in the later 19th century has been remarked by several writers. Clarence Darrow, recalling his common school days, wrote,

> We were taught by our books that we must on all accounts speak the truth; that we must learn our lesson; that we must love our parents and our teacher; must enjoy work; must be generous and kind; must despise riches; must avoid ambition; and then, if we did all these things, some fairy godmother would come along at just the darkest hour and give us everything our hearts desired. (quoted in Tyack, 1967, p. 226)

The boy or girl who would be a good boy or girl had a complex task to accomplish.

Elson (1964) described the common school vision of goodness similarly: "The child is to be religious, industrious, thrifty, persevering, devoted to his parents, obedient to authority, charitable, and chaste; he must also learn to subdue his passions" (p. 212).

Thus, in "Grandfather's Clock" in the *New Education Reader, Book Two*, little May grabs the clock pendulum, stopping the clock. Afraid of a scolding, she decides to tell her mother the truth. The writer advises, "May was a good girl to tell the truth. Good girls tell the truth at all times" (Demarest, 1900, p. 17). In the *New Franklin Third Reader* (Campbell, 1886), the story "Handsome Is as Handsome Does" describes Lucy Gray, much admired by adults; though she is poor, she works hard, helping her mother and cheerfully taking care of younger siblings. Her hands are red and rough, but "[b]eautiful hands are they that do/The work of the noble, good, and true;/Beautiful feet are they that go/swiftly to lighten another's woe" (p. 29).

It is important to note that, despite the instrumental relation of goodness to individual and community advancement, goodness remained, for most of these texts, a benevolence concept. Some texts, for example *McGuffey's Fourth Eclectic Reader* (McGuffey, 1866), carefully distinguished goodness from prudential behavior. In "Circumstances Alter Cases," (pp.224-228) for example, Mr. Derby, wishing to borrow a horse to go to town, asks his neighbor Scrapewell for the loan of his gray mare. Despite the obvious need of his neighbor, Scrapewell puts off all entreaties by inventing excuses for not giving the horse. To every excuse, Derby has a solution, but Scrapewell, all the while describing himself as kind and "more than ready to oblige a friend," invents other excuses (p. 225). Scrapewell even enlists his son Tim to lie that the mare has terribly ripped the skin on her back. Finally, Derby tells the Scrapewells the reason he has to get to town:

> I received a letter this morning from Mr. Griffin, who tells me if I will be in town to-day he will give me the refusal of all that lot of timber, which he is about cutting down, on the side of the hill; and I had intended you should have shared half of it, which would have been not less than fifty dollars in your pocket. But, as your—
> [Scrapewell here interrupts] "Fifty dollars, did you say?" (p. 227).

Suddenly, Scrapewell is truly willing to oblige Derby with the loan of the mare; indeed, he will not take no for an answer. All excuses are made to disappear and Scrapewell sees his neighbor off: "I wish you a good journey and a profitable job" (p. 228). The message is clear enough that the author does not need to take his usual step of tacking it on to the end of the story: It is not goodness that motivated the gift here, but hope of profit. And Scrapewell comes off looking the worse for it.

Goodness had social ramifications, too. There was a tendency in these texts to vary the emphasis on the components of goodness according to a person's "place" in society. Elson (1964) observes that, in these texts, those in superior positions economically and socially (usually indicating superior gifts of character) must, to be good, be charitable and patient toward the poor (who seem also to be the poorer in character in many text examples) and strive to improve their lot. She says of later texts, "The poor are to be treated with benevolence, but not equality" (p. 271). This is at least an improvement from earlier texts, in which benevolent actions toward the poor were sometimes not recommended at all. In Noah Webster's (1831) *American Spelling Book* the question arises whether "when persons are reduced to want by their own laziness and vices, by drunkenness, gambling and the like, is it a duty to relieve them?" He answers, "In general, it is not" (p. 163).

On the other hand, the poor person's goodness, in school texts of the period, often seemed to consist of heroic self-sacrifice, with the hope of miraculous material reward to follow. The story of "The Righteous Never Forsaken" in Ebenezer Porter's (1849) *The Rhetorical Reader* is typical and reminiscent of the Bible's story of Abraham's hospitality to strangers. Here, a very poor widow, about to serve her last herring to her nearly starving young children, finds a stranger on her wintry doorstep, begging for food. She offers to share. The man is astonished: "And is this *all* your store? said he—and a share of this do you offer to one you know not? Then never saw I *charity* before. But madam, do you not wrong your *children* by giving a part of your last mouthful to a stranger?" (p. 153).

The mother refers to her long missing son, gone to be a sailor, saying she'll treat a stranger the way she'd want others to treat her son. But the stranger turns out to be her son, now rich, and they live happily ever after. "God indeed has provided your son a home, and has given him wealth to reward the goodness of his benefactress—my mother! Oh, my mother!" (pp. 153-154).

As the early American benevolence concept of choice, goodness was more often portrayed, as in the previous examples, as a sort of character trait than as a quality of a particular act. It was, as these examples illustrate, a wide-ranging and ill-defined trait as well. Used as a synonym for kindness sometimes; at other times it was seen as involving or consisting of charity, patience, self-sacrifice for the benefit of others, love of humanity, Christian righteousness, and other features more distant from matters of benevolence such as obedience to authority, as noted earlier. Not only must it have been difficult for even willing schoolchildren to figure out how to be good, it must have been continually confusing for them to recognize goodness when they encountered it. Moreover, as the next section will discuss, the uncertain meaning and role of kindness in achieving and demonstrating goodness must have been especially confusing.

There is little doubt that the compilers and disseminators of such texts sincerely believed that if generations of children grew up with such admonitions to goodness, they, and the nation, would prosper. A quick reading of authors/compilers' claims in the prefaces to wide-selling readers of the mid to late 19th and early 20th centuries confirms this assumption. For example, L.H. Jones (1903), the editor of the *Jones Fifth Reader*, prefaces the texts' entries with this remark: "Susceptible as [young adolescents] are at this age to evil influences, they yet respond most readily to the call of higher motives" (p. 3). Ellen M. Cyr's (1901) preface to her *Cyr's Fourth Reader* argues that "[l]iterature in its noblest form should do for the child what it does for the man—open the eyes to clearer vision, and nourish and inspire the soul" (p. v.). Therefore, she concludes, readers have more influence on a student's character than other texts. In *The New Education Reader, Book 4*, from 1901, the preface includes this ambitious promise: "In the choice of selections scrupulous efforts have been made to keep the reading matter absolutely clean in thought, elevating in character, and ennobling in the desires for the highest and best things of earth" (Demarest, 1901, p. 3).

David Tyack and Elizabeth Hansot (1982) noted, "Like a church with its Bible, the rural school with its McGuffey Readers was to be a small incubator of virtue. And as the textbook series most focused on illustrating and arguing for the importance of kindness as a feature of goodness, the *McGuffeys* deserve special attention. Also, it is in these textbooks that confusion over differences among kindness and other related concepts is most evident.

Kindness and Its Relatives in the McGuffey Readers

In the preface to the *Eclectic Primer, Revised* (McGuffey, 1881), the compiler assures teachers and students that "[i]llustrations of the best character have been freely supplied, and the skilled teacher will be able to use them to great advantage" (p. iii). One difficulty, however, for teachers and students intent on developing such character, is the failure of the illustrations to distinguish one desirable moral trait from another. What is presented as examples of kindness, in particular, is often difficult to distinguish from other benevolence-based attributes. Consider, for instance, the following:

1. "This old man can not see. He is blind. Mary holds him by the hand. She is kind to the old blind man" (p. 20). Does this illustrate kindness, or can it just as well be illustrative of Mary caring for the man, or Mary's desire to let the man know she is present, or even Mary's loneliness and wish for connection? Without additional narrative, how are students to learn the differences? Or are they to suppose that any instance of holding a blind man's hand automatically counts as being kind?

2. In this story, one girl lets another hold her doll, and therefore "Sue is kind to Ann" (p. 23). But Sue may be generous in this instance without being kind or she may have an agenda in mind, such as getting Ann to reciprocate or like Sue better. While this last possibility may seem too cynical to mention in such a context, it does illustrate the problem of clarity. After all, as noted earlier, these texts and others of the period took pains to show that goodness begets reward. Can expecting reward be an integral part of goodness?

3. "Tom will not rob a bird's nest. He is too kind to do so" (p. 25). But can this be understood to mean that it is Tom's gentleness that keeps his hand from the nest? His compassion for young birds or babies in general? His rejection of violent acts? What, after all, is the basis for calling his position "kind"?

There are many more and similar examples in this early text of the series, in which kindness is advocated but not clarified. Goodness, after all, is the aim of this moral instruction, since goodness is taken as the hallmark of good character. And goodness in these texts is a hodgepodge of features, benevolent and otherwise. Kindness, whatever it may turn out to be, seems to be but one ill-defined part of the ill-defined notion of goodness.

Other books in the series are filled to bursting with illustrations of and inducements to goodness, many of them purportedly demonstrating kindness. In the *Eclectic First Reader, Revised* (McGuffey, 1879a), there are many narratives of children performing benevolence-related acts toward animals and family members. John gives to Lucy a toy boat he is carving, because she admires it. Meanwhile, Lucy is feeding her hens, for "they must be very hungry by this time" (p. 49). A grandma is described this way: "She is always kind, and takes such good care of me that I like to do what she tells me" (p. 51). Then, "Would you not love a dear, good grandma, who is so kind?" (p. 51). A story advocates treating horses well: "The boys should be kind to their horses. It is not best to whip them" (p. 55).

In all these and other examples, kindness, as part of goodness, is advocated but not clarified. Examples such as these may in fact have led young children to believe that kind acts are always prudential ones. Horses, after all, may perform better for us if we don't whip them.

The *McGuffey* books for older children, both in the "Revised" series and in the "New" series, continued the confusing and conflating presentation of kindness. In the *New Fourth Eclectic Reader* (1866), we find both "The Grateful Indian" and "The Good-Natured Boy." In the first story, a man pays for the dinner of a hungry and wary Indian who had no money. The Indian tells him he will repay his kindness. Years later, he saves the kind man, who has been captured by other Indians. Even less subtly, in the "The Good-Natured Boy" we find Henry, a boy carrying his dinner, relieving the suffering of a dog, a horse, a blind man, and a crippled man; only to be relieved later that day when he is in trouble. Henry repeats several times that "[a] good action is never thrown away" (p. 42).

This last story makes it quite explicit that kind actions inevitably lead to reward, but the story also, by means of its ambiguous title, creates the suggestion either that such kindness is invariably referenced to genetic predisposition, or necessarily tied to a positive mood.

In the *New Fifth Eclectic Reader: Exercises for Schools* (McGuffey, 1886), "The Poor Widow" is sick and sends her young son out to beg. A man, who turns out to be George Washington, helps the boy with money for a doctor and more. The widow recovers and her children grow up to be successful. Here, the text conflates kindness and generosity. In "The Orphan,"

Mr. Lawrence, riding in a stage coach on a cold and rainy night, finds that a young girl is riding outside with the driver. The driver has given her his own coat to keep her warm. Mr. Lawrence brings the girl into the coach, hears her story, and adopts her. Here, we find kindness requiring sacrifice and conflating kindness with pity.

Whether emphasizing goodness or some feature of it, the *McGuffey* books contributed to what seems to have been a widespread belief among school personnel that a vaguely articulated focus on benevolence-motivated acts would help to develop an ideal society. Indeed, some of the most wildly optimistic theorizing in this area found its way explicitly into the *McGuffey* books for older students. In *McGuffey's Newly Revised Rhetorical Guide; or Fifth Reader* (McGuffey, 1853), a piece by Thomas Dick on "Effects of Universal Benevolence" reads, "Were the divine principle of benevolence in full operation among the intelligences that people our globe, this world would be transformed into a paradise" (p. 84). In this piece, Dick proceeds to detail a complete elimination of all inhumane, unjust, cruel, slanderous, murderous, and other immoral actions that would, he thinks, follow the adoption of this "principle of benevolence." The fact that the "principle" in question is never clarified is typical of such arguments.

Without further belaboring the point, it is remarkable that students of the common school era ever gained a consistent and accurate understanding of either the more inclusive notions of benevolence and goodness or the specific feature of goodness promoted as kindness. And without that understanding, it seems impossible for these children to have learned from the texts how to *be* good or kind.

There were, of course, more direct and simply stated references to kindness, its value, and its consequences contained in American school readers. Perhaps the most famous, because most repeated of these pieces, is the *McGuffey Eclectic First Reader's* inclusion of Sarah Hale's poem "Mary's Lamb" (McGuffey, 1836, p. 99). The last stanzas carried an argument about the consequences of kindness to animals: "What makes the lamb love Mary so?'/The eager children cry—/'Oh, Mary loves the lamb, you know'/The Teacher did reply:—/And you each gentle animal/In confidence may bind/And make them follow at your call/If you are always kind." The lesson is clear, even if the meaning of kindness is not. Generations since have evidently believed that the incentive to kindness given in the poem would be important enough to their young children to risk obscuring the rather unfortunate possibility that their kids would try out this kindness routine on lion, tigers, bears, or other less "gentle" and obliging animals.

But the school readers, taken as a whole, introduced a range of settings for and pleasant consequences of kindness. In an early reader, Moses G. Atwood's (1837) *The Progressive Reader or Juvenile Monitor*, the first entry is about "family friendship," in which kindness, hearkening back to its linguistic origins, is illustrated as sharing with siblings, and honoring/respecting behavior toward parents. "People will not speak, or think well of you, if you do not behave kindly to your parents, and to your brothers and sisters," the essay notes (p. 1).

Not surprisingly, the Sunday school movement of the early common school era produced its share of kindness-related literature. In *The Two Sunday School Boys; or The History of Thomas and Joseph* (1832), Thomas, the unrepentant young boy of the story, lies about his behavior quite frequently:

> His lies, however, were generally found out; and although he was frequently warned by his kind teachers of the sad consequences of evil words, and of sinful ways; and was constantly exhorted to pray that God would give him repentance; yet he turned a deaf ear to these wise counsels, and daily became worse and worse (p. 13).

In this text, to be kind is either to display a gentle manner of speech or of action, or, as in the citation, to act or speak with the aim of getting someone else to do what is "good" for him or her—in this case Joseph finishes school at his church thanking his teachers "for their great kindness in teaching him to read the word of God" (p. 16). But Thomas goes from bad to worse, "disregarding the voice of his kind teachers".

In *Lippincott's Fifth Reader* (Wilson, 1881), a text organized around a theme of an "around the world trip," and mixing accounts of the journey with fictional and nonfictional pieces, we find a letter from young Freddy about the great animal hospital in Bombay. Freddy writes to his hometown Society for the Prevention of Cruelty to Animals about it; and chapter members respond with a day of speeches. One speaker begins with a quote from Cowper: "I would not enter on my list of friends/(Though graced with polished manners and fine sense/Yet wanting sensibility) the man/Who needlessly sets foot upon a worm" (p. 359). Here, we are to understand that kindness is to be applied to relations with nonhumans as well. This text follows the preceding episode with an aside to the old story of Androcles and the Lion, in which kindness to an animal is rewarded eventually with kindness from that animal.

Kindness, in these school texts, was often the province of women—when kindness was conflated with gentleness—but some texts made a point of describing a version of kindness suitable for men. In the *New Franklin Fifth Reader* of 1884, Gail Campbell's essay "Manly Tenderness" described for upper-level students what she called "the most cordial and considerate kindness" by men to women (p. 128). Though she reserves "gentleness" for a woman's great adornment, she describes examples of men's everyday kindness in terms of chivalry toward women. She cites men giving "the best seat, the finest standpoint, the warmest corner" to women, coming to the relief of travel-weary women, giving women a hand in slushy weather (p. 128). This describes an overlap with civility, politeness, and gallantry; the differences stemming primarily from the level of conventional behavior involved in determining men's actions. She finds this behavior charming: "It is the wild ivy shooting over the battlements of some old feudal castle, lending grace to solidity" (p. 128).

Some of these texts came closer to the mark in seeing kindness as involving both benevolent attitudes and emotions, but also actions of a certain sort. Henry Ward Beecher's essay in *The Jones Fifth Reader* (Jones, 1903, pp. 159-160) also made a clear distinction between the manner of one's behavior (e.g., gentleness) and actual kindness. In "Character and Reputation" Beecher writes,

[T]here are many men who are reputed to be hard, severe, stern, who at heart are full of all kindness, and would go farther and fare harder to serve a friend or to relieve a real case of trouble than anybody else around them. On the other hand, some people are thought to be very gentle, very sweet in manners, all smiles, promises, and politeness; but at heart they are cold and selfish. (pp. 159-160).

Cyr's Fourth Reader (Cyr, 1901) begins with Abby Morton Diaz's "The Maple Tree's Children," in which a tree is kind to its leaves, which kindly decide to become food to nurture the tree when they fall. Mother Nature kindly makes the death of the leaves in the fall into a lovely scarlet coloring. Here, kindness is presented as involving sacrifice, in the first instance, and thoughtfulness or consideration in the second. This device of using trees, animals, and other nature settings to illustrate kindness was a common strategy in school readers. *The New Education Reader, Book 4*, for instance, include this brief quatrain: "Kind hearts are the gardens/Kind thoughts are the roots/Kind words are the blossoms/Kind deeds are the fruits" (Demarest & Van Sickle, 1901). And *The Expressive Third Reader* (Baldwin & Bender, 1901) included A. Segerstedt's "The Little Plant," a fable of how the sun and rain arrange to help a fragile little plant survive and prosper after other creatures in the woods had abused the plant. The fable finishes with "[a]nd a little bird said, 'It is better to be kind and gentle than rude and unmannerly" (pp. 125–126).

It is clear that, by the last decades of the 19th century, a substantial body of intellectuals in this country were so restless with a moral emphasis for education that they saw this emphasis as at best contrived and at worst misleading, in a world they saw through a gradually more pessimistic naturalist perspective. One of Mark Twain's (1870) lesser-known pieces uses a mock-astonished tone to frame a cynical attitude toward such schoolbook goodness:

> Once there was a good little boy by the name of Jacob Blivens. He always obeyed his parents, no matter how absurd their demands were. . . . He would not play hookey, even when his sober judgment told him it was the most profitable thing he could do. None of the other boys could ever make that boy out, he acted so strangely. . . . He wouldn't play marbles on Sunday, he wouldn't rob birds' nests, he wouldn't give hot pennies to organ-grinders' monkeys; he didn't seem to take any interest in any kind of rational amusement.
>
> This good little boy . . . believed in the good little boys they put in the Sunday-school books; he had every confidence in them. He longed to come across one of them alive, once; but he never did. They all died before his time, maybe.
>
> But somehow, nothing ever went right with this good little boy; nothing ever turned out with him the way it always turned out with the good little boys in the books. They always had a good time, and the bad boys had the broken legs; but in his case there was a screw

loose somewhere, and it all happened just the other way. . . . And once, when some bad boys pushed a blind man over in the mud, and Jacob ran to help him up and receive his blessing, the blind man did not give him any blessing at all, but whacked him over the head with his stick and said he would like to catch him shoving *him* again and then pretending to help him up. This was not in accordance with any of the books. Jacob looked them all over to see.

Finally, when Jacob, who knows from the texts he aspires to emulate that he is to be kind to animals, is "around hunting up bad little boys to admonish, he found a lot of them in the old iron foundry fixing up a little joke on fourteen or fifteen dogs, which they had tied together in a long procession and were going to ornament with empty nitro-glycerine cans made fast to their tails." Jacob knows at once that he is supposed to intervene, so he sits on those nitro cans and warns the boys off. They do run off, but only because the Alderman McWelter comes in, angry. The only boy left is Jacob, and the Alderman doesn't wait to hear Jacob's pretty speech:

He took Jacob Blivens by the ear and turned him around, and hit him a whack in the rear with the flat of his hand; and in an instant that good little boy shot out through the roof and soared away toward the sun, with the fragments of those fifteen dogs stringing after him like the tail of a kite. And . . . although the bulk of him came down all right in a tree-top in an adjoining county the rest of him was apportioned around among four townships, and so they had to hold five inquests on him to find out whether he was dead or not, and how it occurred. You never saw a boy scattered so.

So perished the good little boy who did the best he could, but didn't come out according to the books. Every boy who ever did as he did prospered, except him. His case is truly remarkable. It will probably never be accounted for. (as quoted in McElderry, 1965, pp. 44–46).

So might perish as well, Twain seems to have hoped, the idea that this difficult, complex, and shifting notion of goodness might be worth striving for as a paradigm of moral functioning.

Still, school texts of the era, although they failed to provide clear and consistent accounts of kindness, took all they thought of as kindness very seriously. For this age of American schooling, kindness, no matter how unclearly defined, was not supererogatory. It was a moral imperative that, however vague its dimensions, was seen as a necessary feature of a civilized, productive human being and of real importance to a growing democratic nation. My arguments, in the chapters that follow, may be considered, in part, to be in the service of updating and clarifying similar beliefs.

CHAPTER TWO

THE MEANING OF KINDNESS

AS CHAPTER 1 ARGUES, kindness, at least at first glance, is ill-defined and so is not a promising term in which to incorporate some consistent approach to a teaching ethic. Ill-defined moral terms seem unlikely candidates to be useful bases for moral programs. Thomas Aquinas, speaking of a term related to kindness, famously wrote, "I would rather feel compassion than know the meaning of it". The temptation to avoid a messy analysis is a strong one, and the popular websites that today advocate for increasing acts of kindness tend to share Aquinas's approach.

Even so, there is coherent core meaning in the term "kindness," and I will try to draw it out. Moreover, the term's very familiarity and fuzziness make it a good candidate for cooptation, which I will also, in some respects, do here—just as terms such as "caring," "hospitality," and "tact" have been taken over and partly reconstructed by other writers (for instance, Noddings, 1984 and Von Manen, 2016). It seems useful, to speak clearly of the sort of features that mark a useful teaching ethic, to use a term that in large measure actually captures the key features of my concern, and to stipulate a clear account of the term for those parts which are, in ordinary use, not clear at all. My account of kindness will be, for the most part, an attempt at an accurate conceptual analysis, but also, in part, a construct. Even so, the account is one aimed at providing clarity.

Kindness and Its Kin

Though the concept of kindness is from time to time discussed as a sort of character trait, or as a virtue, or even as a presidential ethos (we remember President Bush, Sr.'s call for a "kinder, gentler nation"), the more usual context for noticing kindness is in a particular act or situation. Though popular treatments of kindness seem often to assume that both the concept and acts of kindness are simple to recognize, in this chapter I will argue otherwise. There are a number of essential features we must recognize in acts and situations to distinguish them as ones of kindness as opposed to related attributions—and it is important to make such distinctions to see, ultimately, the value of a teaching ethic that is centered in kindness. Drawing on a range of examples, including some of those described in chapter one, we discover that recognizing kindness requires that we see certain relational, intentional/emotional, knowledge/belief, and success features at work in a given situation. The following sections cover these in more detail.

Relational Features

Some of the features that distinguish kindness from other concepts have to do with the ways in which the one acting kindly (K) "meets" the one to whom the kind act is directed (the recipient R). These relational features include

1. that there is a particular R (set of R's) toward whom K acts;

2. that there is a particular occasion in which K acts toward R;

3. that K, in the situation at hand, is in a position to affect some need of R;

4. that some need on the part of R actually exists and that K's action relates to addressing that need; and

5. that K avoids, to a significant extent, what Noddings (1984) calls "motivational displacement."

Feature one calls attention to the fact that, in acting kindly, there is a one-to-one quality about what happens. As opposed to related concepts such as charity, which may be directed to whole populations at a time and without focus on any persons specifically and singly, kindness seems to require that we focus on particular persons (though we may also be kind to animals, the focus here is on persons). Though a teacher may certainly be kind, on some occasions, to some students, as when the teacher gives some of them extra time and help with a crucial assignment with which students are struggling, to call such an act "kind" seems to imply that the teacher's relationship is with each student personally.

Feature two recognizes that, unlike what is necessary to such concepts as caring or fidelity, acts of kindness are discrete ones, rather than part of an ongoing relationship. I may act kindly toward a student even if that or another kind act on my part toward that student never again occurs. To be sure, some K may act kindly toward some R numerous times, but each act is recognizable as kind without the necessity of linking each act. So, I may meet a student numerous times after school to help the student with her need to catch up with the rest of the class. Each meeting may constitute a kind act, and those actions as a discrete set might also count as kind action. If, however, I was recognizable as caring for the student in my work with her, what is implied is an ongoing (though not necessarily a permanent) relationship with the student. Still, we do recognize individuals as kind persons, and this at least implies that such a person can, to a large degree, be relied on, or has a tendency to behave kindly in situations described in this chapter; and this book argues for the importance of being or becoming a kind teacher.

Feature three speaks to relative power in the situation. We can't speak of someone acting kindly if that person is powerless to affect someone else's position. If a teacher, for instance, is not competent to provide the help a student needs, no act of the teacher with regard to that need could be called kind. This feature does not address the general relative power status of K and R but refers instead to K's power to affect R's need. Though teachers have a "higher" general status in the school than a student, a student may still, on occasion, perform a kind act toward a teacher. Put another way, in comparing kindness with related terms such as "mercy," it is clear that in concepts such as mercy, R must be *in* someone's power; but in kindness, K *must have the power* to affect R's position. With mercy, the one receiving it is dependent on the merciful one's action; failing the merciful act, the recipient has no recourse. We should also note that this power to help need not mean that K sacrifices power or K's own general welfare in acting kindly. While a kind act may come at cost to some K, that need not be the case. If a teacher finds a student's lost pen on the floor and returns it, that act may, in some instances, be a kind one even if it comes with no cost to the teacher and bestows no added power on the student in relation to the teacher. With generosity, in contrast, what is given must be seen as a sacrifice, to some degree, on the part of the one acting generously. It is also true that an act may be *both* kind and generous, as when the teacher gives a student who is hungry and without funds for a meal enough money to buy that meal. If the need is real, the funding may meet all the conditions for kindness described in this chapter and be a generous sacrifice of the teacher's own wherewithal, too. If the funding really wasn't needed by the student, or the student didn't really need the meal, the teacher's act could still be generous, if not kind.

The "need" mentioned in feature four refers to some situation which, left unaddressed, would actually cause harm to R (but see chapter five for some problems with the notion of need). This is not to be confused with R's desires—with things R believes would gratify him or her. To act with regard to R's desires that are not also needs may help to make one's act considerate, generous, hospitable, indulgent, "nice," or accommodating, but would disqualify one from being kind. As an example, if a teacher recognizes that one of his students would like to but doesn't need to leave class early to speak with the principal and the teacher allows the student to go, that would be considerate, generous, or accommodating but not kind. If the student really needed to leave, however, the teacher's act, all other features being in place, would be recognizable as a kind act.

The notion of need presents problems of perspective for identifying acts of kindness. From the point of view of a potential K, a potential R may have a need, as defined, that the potential recipient of K's act may not be aware of and may even deny having, even to the point of resenting what K sees as a kind act toward him or her. Moreover, other observers of the situation may or may not recognize that need and therefore will fail to see K's act as kind. Some acts that purport to address a need become controversial because the need is one that can't, by its logical nature, be verified. An important example of this last situation has to do with true believers in a religious or otherwise metaphysical doctrine attempting to proselytize a person so as to "save" him or her. Those who are devout may see those actions as kind, while others, not recognizing that a need exists, may see the actions as coercive, or at best patronizing; and verifying such a need would be impossible (though faith may fill the evidential gap).

A "situation that . . . would cause harm to R," it should be noted, can refer also to a vulnerability that R has. For example, teachers who work with students with disabilities can act kindly, *ceteris paribus*, when they act to mitigate effects of those disabilities. Or a teacher, recognizing how a student with a low self-image will react to other students teasing him or her, might be recognized as acting kindly when the teacher proactively discourages such teasing.

At the least, identifying need can require, on the part of K, insight, occasionally research, and usually a level of observation of and communication with R. William Hamrick (2002) notes that "[k]indness is a way of knowing the other as other, because it requires both closeness and distance, proximity and tactful differentiation, compassionate intervention and appropriate withdrawal" (pp. 68–69). This characterization applies even to the situation in which a potential R actually asks for help from a potential K. Teachers are very familiar with such situations—even wishing that students would ask for help more often. But such occasions still require, for the teacher, the insight, observation, familiarity and distance needed to evaluate the student's situation before acting in a way that could be recognized as kind.

The second clause of feature four speaks to the relation of K's *action* to R's need, rather than to a more general connection of K to R. Many actions taken by one person may affect the need of another person by accident or incidentally without being kind. A teacher might relieve one student's experience of being bullied by another student when the teacher arranges for the bully to be expelled, even though the teacher's actions were addressed to the bully's situation without thought to the one bullied. In an act we recognize as kind, we see K addressing R's need.

Clearly, the relations between K and R, no matter how limited by the context of K's action, are complex. In this and other ways, kind acts are rarely simple ones to accomplish or to recognize.

Finally, feature five introduces one of the most important considerations in any discussion of the importance of kindness to a teaching ethic: the presence of multiple perspectives in K's decision to act. Though I will discuss this feature more at length later on, it is necessary in speaking of relational conditions of kindness to observe that an act is not kind if the *only* perspective from which possible decisions are considered is that of R's need. Though it may be symptomatic of caring (or the care ethicist's construction of that term) that the one caring adopts the motivations of the one cared for in deciding what to do, I will argue that to recognize kindness, we must at least observe that K takes on multiple perspectives in the situation at hand, including R's, K's, and those of others who may be seriously affected by K's actions. We should also note that an act done in consideration only of the relative needs of all those affected by the act relates to a concern for justice.

Finally, an act whose motivation is solely to deal with the needs of the one acting is prudential. Phillips and Taylor (2010) note that the modern post-Hobbesian view has it that self-interest, morally, is primary, making kindness itself either self-serving or a moral weakness. But in practice, we recognize that kind acts are moral ones and always involve more than self-interest. A kind act relates to the needs of K, R, and others who may be affected by what K does in the name of R's need (see the story of Dr. Joan and Martha, later in this chapter, for an illustration).

Intentional and Emotional Features

In acting kindly,

1. K intends to show respect for R's position, and in fact feels respect for R's position;

2. it is K's intention to act in such a way that R's need is met;

3. K's actions are voluntary; and

4. K's actions are discretionary.

In feature one, when we notice that K attends to R's need but in a manner that trivializes that need, we recognize condescension. This is not to say that K must respect R, like R, or admire R. Kind acts are not acts of worship, of love, or of friendship (though such states of affairs may inspire kind acts). A teacher need not have affection toward a student or think highly of that student to act kindly toward him or her. But a teacher, or any K, must believe that R's situation, and the need it has created for R, is worthy of K's response.

There is some debate over the question of whether certain emotions in K must be present to recognize K's action toward R as kind. Must K have compassion toward R and R's need? Is it more correct to say that K must empathize with R in R's situation?

What at least is clear is that acting kindly does not require acting in a kindly manner. It is not difficult to have noted at one time or another some person of a usually cold demeanor who has acted in a way toward some R that we recognize as kind—even if that K acts toward R in a manner that seems hard or cold. The 19th-century minister Henry Ward Beecher, in a piece appearing in the *Jones Fifth Reader* (Jones, 1903) called "Character and Reputation," notes this fact. Here, Beecher distinguishes between the two concepts of the piece's title.

> [T]here are many men who are reputed to be hard, severe, stern, who at heart are full of all kindness, and would go farther and fare harder to serve a friend or to relieve a real case of trouble than anybody else around them. On the other hand, some people are thought to be very gentle, very sweet in manners, all smiles, promises, and politeness; but at heart they are cold and selfish."

But to say that "at heart" someone is disposed to recognize and address others' needs is still problematic because it fails to distinguish between emotional terms such as "compassion" on the one hand and cognitive terms such as "recognition" and "intention" on the other.

"Empathy," an alternative term to consider, here, is unfortunately used ambiguously in just the ways that point to the emotional/cognitive divide: We sometimes talk of empathy in situations in which we note a recognition of someone else's circumstance or that person's responses to the situation. But psychologists and human development researchers (see, for instance, Nancy Eisenberg, et al., 2006) identify empathy as both an inherited and learned emotional response in reaction to others' situations.

Though empathy, like compassion, is usually seen as at least a causal factor in beneficent acts, empathy is not universally praised for its role in some kinds of moral judgments. Some writers take the view that moral decision-making, especially when it affects the larger community's welfare, should avoid a reliance on empathy. Paul Bloom (quoted in Cameron, Inzlicht, and Cunningham, 2015), evidently basing such a claim on research that found people show more empathy toward individuals they know than toward groups or strangers, said that empathy is a "parochial, narrow-minded emotion," one that "will have to yield to reason if humanity is to survive" (p. 12).

The tendency to conflate terms such as "kindness," "compassion," and "empathy" is marked in modern usage. Daniel Goleman's (2012) attempt to describe "compassionate acts" is typical: "If empathy arises, and if that person is in dire need, then empathic concern can come. You want to help them, and then that begins a compassionate act". But it is not clear that having compassion for someone in need must lead to actions of any sort. Mixing emotions, desires, recognition, actions, and more, such an account confuses more than it clarifies.

It seems clear that kind actions are very often accompanied and influenced by compassionate or empathetic emotions (or by pity, for that matter). Yet it also seems often to be the case that a kind act may be accomplished by a K who simply reasons that, in the situation at hand, an R's need, once identified, is worthy of being addressed. In some broad sense, it seems at least correct to say that, in acting kindly, K must believe R's need to be deserving of mitigation, that is, worthy of respect. A.D.M. Walker (1989) writes that "[u]nderlying the kind person's response to others is a view of them as vulnerable, as liable to be hurt by the way in which they are treated" (p. 353). And it may well be the case that this belief may have cognitively developed origins, emotional ones, or both.

With feature two, though I will argue that one acting kindly always intends to regard the interest of people other than R, still, K must at least intend to address R's need. This distinguishes kindness from concepts such as tact, in which the tactful person's concern is to avoid having someone's need arise at all, exacerbating the need he or she sees, or to not call it to public attention (though there are occasions when not calling R's situation to people's attention may also be kind). Moreover, one way we recognize acts as *opposites* of kindness is by the lack of this feature. When someone acts with no intention to respect the need of another person, in circumstances that we believe call for that regard, we call that act *un*kind, and when someone acts so as to frustrate someone else in meeting his or her need, or so as to aggravate that need, we call it cruel.

Also, kind acts offer a sort of counterweight in this respect, to what we might term "formalized-intention" acts, such as ones of courtesy, politeness, etiquette, and so on. These formalized acts may aim to provide good outcomes for someone but without the intention to address the specific needs of those they aim to help. Indeed, formalized-intention acts do not even require what I will shortly describe as act-relevant, detailed knowledge of R's needs, nor do they require insight into possible effects of the act on others affected by it. On the other hand, some writers on etiquette, courtesy, and politeness insist on seeing these notions as what Elizabeth Post (1975) calls "a code of behavior, *based on consideration and kindness*, and manners [that] are the outward evidence that we live by that code" (p. vii, emphasis added). So, if a teacher responds to a student's outburst in class with a courteous reply that the teacher has come to recognize helps to calm the student and shows respect to the student's situation, the courtesy the teacher shows can be seen as a kind act. Still, to insist that courteous acts must, to deserve that name, be based in kindness, seems an overreach. Many polite or courteous acts are pro forma only, though they may be appreciated nonetheless by their recipient.

William Hamrick (2002) also notes another "opposite" of a kind act—one that is inconsiderate. In such an act, the one acting fails to be aware of someone's need or desires (as opposed to an unkind act, where the one acting is so aware) and acts in a way that does not help to address the need or desire in a situation where the needful one or someone else believes the need/desire should have been noticed and addressed. While we recognize that very young children often act in this manner because they aren't developmentally and/or experientially ready to look for and correctly identify R's need, and thus we do not see their actions as inconsiderate, we are not so forgiving in judging those we believe "should have known better." This observation relates also to what, later, I will call "knowledge" features of kindness.

Feature three relates to a Scottish proverb, which insists that "[k]indness comes o'will: it canna be coft [bought]." If a teacher's contract requires him or her to help keep the school's hallways picked up, then doing so is not a kind act, though it benefits those who tread the halls. If a teacher is coerced by a principal or parent into staying after school to help a student with assignments, the teacher's actions in doing so are not kind, even if they do attend to a need. Likewise, if we believe that a teacher has become obsessed with a student, we will not count that teacher's many helpful actions toward that student as kind if we see those actions as emanating from the obsession.

In feature four, K must feel that viable alternative choices of action are available rather than the one chosen. If an act is done because the actor feels there is no other choice, or if one acts because convention or ritual demands it, that act may be doing the right thing; "proper" behavior; common decency; or even, from another perspective, righteous, but it can't be kind. There is some irony, for instance, in a situation where a teacher feels she has no choice but to help a student because her religion requires that followers must act kindly toward others.

Kant (1785/2013), in the *Metaphysics of Morals*, argues that what gives an act its moral worth is that it is done as a duty, in conformance to a universalizable principle. In using the golden rule as an example, he notes that love, as affection, can't be "commanded," "but beneficence for duty's sake may". Once we recognize an act as a duty, we are self-commanded.

But duty, as it happens, can be understood in several ways, neither of which can be the origin of a kind act. If duty is imposed from without, it is clear that an act emanating from that outside control would not be kind because it is not voluntary. Indeed, if writers such as John Wilson, Williams, and Sugarman (1967) are correct, acting in this context would arguably not be a moral act at all. If the sense of duty is instead internal in origin, how we see the act depends on whether the act's motivation was primarily to help with R's need, or on the other hand primarily to maintain the integrity of the self-imposed duty. If the first, we may see the act as kind; if the second, we see the act as, in a curious way, prudential—done primarily for self-benefit, as creating a sense of self-justification or pleasure.

If the teacher acts because he or she feels he or she has no discretion in the matter, her act is not a kind one, no matter its effects. In general, kind acts are not intended to respond conventionally in any way to the situation at hand, even if the act does in fact correspond to a conventional response. Kind acts' dependence on multiple perspectives ensures that each is, to an extent, demanding of a unique response. This is not to say, however, that helping acts done from unreflective habits or that ingrained in us by previous teaching are not valuable in dealing with others' needs. Heinrich Fichtenau (1991), writing about 10th-century mentality, writes that "[w]e should not underestimate the pedagogical effect of the constant practice of conduct prescribed by habit. What we dismiss as mere etiquette had a certain formative power" (p. 4). There are other positive moral concepts, motivations, and actions than those having to do with kindness.

Knowledge and Belief Features

What makes an act kind includes features that describe certain beliefs and abilities:

1. K believes that R actually has a need and K understands R's situation and need.

2. K knows how to address R's need and how to do so with regard to the multiple perspectives relevant to the situation.

With feature one, if a potential K fails to recognize that a potential R has a need, no action that the actor takes toward the recipient, even if it accidentally addresses that recipient's need, would be recognized as a kind act. For example, if a teacher walking down the street notices a $20 bill on the ground by a man standing nearby, and, thinking that the bill probably belongs to that man, picks it up and hands it to him, that act is certainly polite; but if it turns out the recipient is starving (perhaps it is another teacher, given current salaries) and without money and the windfall $20 enables him to buy food, would we call the giving of that bill a kind act? The act would certainly be a beneficent, courteous one, but not a kind one if the giver was unaware of the recipient's need.

While we may from time to time benefit from the kindness of strangers, a stranger must at least be able to gain some insight into the particular nature of our need, to be said to act kindly toward us. Strangers may act in conventional ways that help us, without particular knowledge of our situation, but that again would be courtesy rather than kindness. A teacher may have enough experience with other students in similar situations to make a shrewd guess at the need of a student with whom the teacher is not well acquainted, and a teacher may come to know a particular student well enough to guess correctly at a current need. Some such knowledge seems required to distinguish kind acts toward those students from accidental or incidental aid on the one hand and courtesy and politeness on the other. Moreover, a potential K can only judge his or her potential act's effect on R's need and on other affected parties by means of K's level of informed deliberation. The more K knows of R and of R's need, and of the potential effects of K's act on others affected by it, the greater the chance that the act will both successfully address R's need and be recognized as kind. Kindness implies understanding.

For feature two an extended example may help for illustration. Martha, a student in Dr. Joan's class, is having a bad day. Though not normally disruptive, today she is talking to herself, ignoring Joan, and disturbing the concentration of her neighbors. Finally, Dr. Joan asks her to quiet down, to which Martha replies in a loud voice, "I won't!" The class looks and sounds shocked by this behavior; all eyes turn to Dr. Joan.

Dr. Joan realizes that something is wrong with Martha. Something very disturbing must have occurred to make her act this way, since it is so different from what Dr. Joan is familiar with and since Dr. Joan notices obvious signs in Martha of emotional distress. From what she has been hearing from other teachers, Dr. Joan suspects that Martha's parents are breaking up and that this has much to do with Martha's current behavior.

To act kindly toward Martha in this situation, Dr. Joan must consider the problem from more than just the perspective of Martha's situation and Martha's needs. She must also consider her own situation: how attending to Martha's emotional and other needs may affect her own position with the class at this moment and in the foreseeable future. Dr. Joan must also consider the welfare of the rest of the class in her choice of how to meet Martha's needs on this occasion: how will Joan's actions affect what they learn today, their emotional states, their satisfaction with the class, and more?

To leave out any of these perspectives—even though her main concern is to see to Martha's welfare—is to keep Dr. Joan's eventual actions from being kind ones. If Dr. Joan acts only from the perspective of meeting Martha's needs, we may recognize caring, thoughtfulness, consideration, or a number of other benevolent acts, but not kindness. If Dr. Joan acts only from the point of view of her own interests, she acts prudentially, perhaps incidentally in a way that will help Martha, but not kindly. If Dr. Joan's perspective is entirely that of what would be best for the entire class, she may act in a way that we see as aspiring to be fair or just, but not as kind.

What might Joan do to act kindly toward Martha, acting with knowledge of the situation that encompasses the effects of her act on the welfare of those importantly affected by her act? Her task, if her act is to be a kind one, is to find a way to meet Martha's needs in the context of her own interests and of the welfare of the class as a whole. There may be a number of ways to proceed. One way might be to take a moment to get the rest of the class working on a task relevant to the lesson at hand and then move to Martha's desk to quietly ask questions and suggest alternatives that Martha may find soothing and useful. In this way, Joan's need to keep the lesson moving is met, the rest of the class benefits (unless, of course, those students spend most of their time trying to listen to the conversation Joan is having with Martha), and Martha's immediate need is addressed without her being humiliated in front of the class. If all this is accomplished, we will probably see Joan's actions as kind ones.

It may be objected that here I am asking of kindness more than is reflected in ordinary usage. We speak, after all of "simple acts of kindness," don't we? And the concept I am outlining is not simple, but quite complex. My response (leaving aside the point that, as a construct, this notion of kindness is intended to provide a vehicle for articulating a program for building a teaching ethic) is that our actual understanding of kindness is a complex concept. That is why it is possible to distinguish it along many lines from related and contrasting concepts.

A note about a role for R's response in identifying kindness: The story of Dr. Joan and Martha may suggest to readers a question about Martha's response to Dr. Joan's actions: Must Martha recognize and appreciate Dr. Joan's actions to see those actions as kind? The answer is that Martha must recognize Dr. Joan's intent, and the action's success in addressing a need; but she is not required to appreciate Dr. Joan's efforts. In fact, Martha may, in some situations, recognize Dr. Joan's actions as kind and yet be entirely unappreciative of them. Martha may resent the fact that Dr. Joan took it on herself to respond to a need that Martha recognizes but didn't want Joan to intervene with. This sort of "benefit paternalism" may be seen by some, and by its recipient, as kind but not appreciated.

The Success Condition

Finally, to say that an act is kind appears to impute a sort of success to the act. We say sometimes that an act was intended to be kind but was not. Often what is meant is that the act did not meet R's need or that it created other and important problems for R, even if it met the original need—including new problems for R that stem from the harm that helping R caused for others affected by K's actions. To illustrate, if, in the case of Martha and her teacher Dr. Joan, Dr. Joan's attempt to meet Martha's need should result in members of the class feeling that Dr. Joan was favoring Martha to the exclusion of other members of the class, and should classmates then ostracize Martha, we would not see Joan's actions toward Martha as kind—even if kindly intended.

It is worth noting, although with a degree of skepticism, that some writers claim kindness is in general unsuccessful, in the sense that it is, by its nature, paternalistic and therefore harmful to its recipients (see Dworkin, 1972; Mill, 1859/2002). The claim is that doing something "for someone's own good" or to prevent the recipients' self-harm preempts autonomy, which presumably is a higher good.

It is noted that kind acts need not be appreciated by their recipients. When a teacher or administrator makes a decision to retain a student for another year in the same grade, the student or the parents of the student are often resentful. Still, the act may be recognized by others as kind and also successful in meeting a need that its recipients may not appreciate at the time, but that others, such as teachers, see, from their multiple perspectives, as paramount for both the student and others affected by the act.

For any choice we may make, our ability to foresee its consequences is limited; the legal notion of proximate cause has application, here. Kind acts have long-term consequences and may address long-term needs, even if a particular R or others do not recognize that need immediately. These critics' argument forces us to recognize that, as educators, we teach in part with an eye to longer-term, even ideal aims, as I will discuss in a later chapter. And these aims, though they may include levels of autonomy as important goals for our students, may also or instead include, and even give precedence to, community-oriented aims, though these may not be currently important to some students or parents; or these aims may be for students' material well-being, even if at present some students have no materialistic objectives. Community needs are part of the multiple perspectives a K may see as relevant in acting kindly. Moreover, it is often the case that teachers recognize student needs before their students do. Addressing those needs, especially in situations of potential danger to students (either immediate or long term), is not paternalistic, though the recipients of such kindness may not be appreciative of it or have a say in whether it should have been done.

The point in noting this "success" feature of the concept and of acting kindly, and of the other features mentioned earlier, is that acting kindly is not simply a complex activity; it is also a skilled activity. If teachers are to work toward a teaching ethic that stresses acting kindly toward their students and other clients, the work they have before them will require a number of abilities—performative, propositional, and dispositional. But then, teaching successfully in general is a considerably more complex and skilled activity than the common wisdom about teaching supposes.

CHAPTER THREE

SENSIBILITY AND THE LOGIC OF ETHICAL JUDGMENT

IN ARGUING, AS I will in this book, for kindness as a central feature of educators' professional ethical relationships with their clientele, it is necessary to describe how kindness is actualized in teachers' professional decision making. That, in turn, requires an account of how moral judgments are made, in which it becomes clear how an emphasis on kindness affects and is affected by ethical judgment. Just as kindness itself is a complex concept, and just as kind acts involve a complex of features, it turns out that ethical judgments involve a wider range of features than are traditionally assumed.

Singular ethical judgements, I will argue, are to a large extent and on most occasions determined by what I will term, to borrow a centuries-old concept, a person's "ethical sensibility."

Much moral philosophy since Kant, and much American writing about moral education perhaps since we were colonies, has oversimplified and over-systematized the task of understanding what goes on when we make moral choices. I want to use the occasion of noticing certain developments in neuroscience to begin to describe a process of moral decision making and moral action that complicates matters considerably, both generally and in professional ethical judgments.

In this complicating process, I also borrow from and attempt to draw connections among work not only in neuroscience, but also in philosophy, psychology, fiction and literary theory, and other fields concerned with moral choice. I ask readers to reconsider the primarily 18th-century notion of sensibility and its modern descendants. Beginning with accounts by David Hume (1777/1965) and Adam Smith (1776/1976), I attempt to resurrect and reformulate the role of sensibility in making individual ethical choices. I believe that a version of this concept will provide a useful touchstone for understanding the processes of moral deliberation and moral choice.

In reconsidering sensibility as the key to understanding the moral/ethical judgments and choices we make, I have been motivated in part by the curious attractiveness of the term in certain literary and journalistic circles. The *New York Times*, for several decades, and especially in its section on the arts, has used the term frequently, in ways its writers don't seem to want to unpack. In reviews of the arts, critics at the *Times* describe such concepts as "an old world sensibility" (4/01/2015 p. C1), or a "a buyer with the literary sensibility" (11/4/2002m p. C8), or even a "worrywart sensibility (5/2/2011, p. C1). While most mentions of the term don't directly address moral issues, this modern usage begs analysis that I believe will connect it intimately with the moral arguments we make and the choices of moral action to which we arrive.

My long-term aim for this inquiry is a reformulation of approaches to moral education that are based in the ways people actually deal with moral issues. Though that educational purpose is not the main concern of this chapter, it is with that task in mind that I attempt these foundational arguments.

Sensibility in Moral Choice

In a study reported in *Science* (Greene, Sommerville, Nystrom, Darley, & Cohen, 2001), researchers set out to use modern tools of brain research and new findings about the neural correlates of emotional response to shed some light on a puzzling finding that stemmed from responses to a class of moral dilemmas. In an example of this dilemma, two seemingly parallel situations are presented to subjects for judgment; in the first situation,

a runaway trolley is headed for five people who will be killed if it continues on its present course. The only way to save them is to hit a switch that will turn the trolley onto an alternate set of tracks where it will kill one person instead of five. Ought you to turn the trolley in order to save five people at the expense of one? (p. 2105)

Almost all those faced with this dilemma judge that switching the trolley onto the alternate tracks is an appropriate decision. However, when faced with a dilemma seemingly quite parallel to the trolley case, almost all those responding to it judge otherwise:

As before, a trolley threatens to kill five people. You are standing next to a large stranger on a footbridge that spans the tracks, in between the oncoming trolley and the five people. In this scenario, the only way to save the five people is to push this stranger off the bridge, onto the tracks below. He will die if you do this, but his body will stop the trolley from reaching the others. Ought you to save the five others by pushing this stranger to his death? (p. 2106)

In this case, almost all respondents say this choice is not acceptable. Why is it judged acceptable to sacrifice one for five in the trolley case but not in the footbridge case?

In the Greene and colleagues (2001) experiment, the researchers found that, by presenting these and other similar cases to subjects while using functional MRI scanning to detect activity in areas of the brain associated with emotional response, one factor that has an effect on people's judgment is emotional engagement (described physiologically), in some cases but not in others. When presented with what the researchers called "moral-personal" cases like that of the footbridge—which involved the prospect of directly and personally inflicting serious physical harm on a particular person—areas of the brain associated with emotional response, specifically areas associated with sadness and fright, became active. But when presented with "moral-impersonal" cases in which the criteria did not apply—such as the trolley case, decisions about keeping money found in a lost wallet, or voting for a policy expected to cause more deaths than its alternatives—these emotional centers were not activated, though areas of the brain associated with working memory were significantly more active than for the moral-personal cases.

Additionally, the researchers found that, for those rare respondents who judged the sacrifice of one for five appropriate in the footbridge case, there was noticeable hesitation or interference in making this judgment, a phenomenon similar to that observed by Stroop (1935). Stroop found that people's ability to say "green" in situations where they observed the word "red" written in green was delayed. The researchers in the Greene and colleagues' (2001) study concluded from this and from their findings about emotional engagement that "the increased emotional responses generated by the moral-personal dilemmas have an influence on and are not merely incidental to moral judgment" (p. 2107).

The researchers stress that their findings in no way show that it is emotional response that *determines* moral judgment; nor do their findings actually identify beyond doubt just what it is in certain cases that provokes the physiological response observed. Indeed, other researchers have begun to observe and describe a complex and, to an extent, an individualized brain-based process that takes us from sensory input to moral judgement and action (for an accessible summary, see Zull, 2002).

Greene's later work has provided some degree of response to some of these questions. In reporting follow-up research on the emotional basis of personal moral decisions, Greene (2004) notes that in many personal moral judgments there is conflicting activation in brain areas associated with both cognitive reasoning and emotional response. This occurs in situations in which there are "difficult personal moral dilemmas in which utilitarian values require 'personal' moral violations" (p. 389). Greene says that a personal moral violation is "ME HURT YOU"—where we contemplate action that is likely to cause "serious bodily harm" to a particular person or persons that the actor him- or herself is directly responsible for from the agent's will (p. 389).

Greene's previous research found personal moral judgments that are associated with brain areas of emotion and cognitive brain areas more active in impersonal moral judgments. But when subjects judged personal moral violations to be appropriate, those judgments took longer than when violations were judged inappropriate. This, Greene, et al. (2001) found, was because such violations, to be judged appropriate, had to engage cognitive control over emotional response.

Interestingly, Greene's (2004) findings supported the view that in difficult personal moral dilemmas, brain activation tends to favor utilitarian cognitive judgment over emotional judgment. One example of what Greene called a difficult personal moral judgment was the "crying baby" case, in which the choice is over whether to smother a crying baby to stop the sounds from exposing a group of people hiding from enemy soldiers who will kill them all. Greene provides, as an example of an "easy" personal dilemma, the decision of whether to kill a newborn unwanted baby.

I will take up in a later chapter Greene's and others' research on factors that lead those making singular moral judgments to adopt cognitively based decision making practices over purely emotional bases for singular moral judgments (Greene, 2014; Paxton, Ungar, & Greene, 2012, Greene et al., 2001,). This research seems to provide an entry point for instruction that could lead educators and others to handle the often complex factors that go into acting kindly.

For moral philosophy, however, findings such as these are provocative. One obvious problem it suggests is for any attempt to systematically describe moral judgment as proceeding from moral principles, whether categorical or prima facie. A "logic" of moral judgment will clearly have to account at least for psychological and physiological factors.

These findings also suggest other questions for those attempting to both describe the process of moral judgment and to consider ways in which education may affect such judgment: What should be identified as a "moral" judgment? Is it one not only focused on our actions' effects on the welfare of others, but also one that provokes emotional engagement? How should we characterize the situation types that engage emotions—as ones in which we anticipate personal agency in potential physical harm to others? As any in which we are able to apply the visceral notion of potential "harm," even if it is not physical harm? Are these situation types ones that universally engage emotions, or is this engagement constrained by certain factors? What factors might these be—maturational and individual inheritance factors? Sociocultural and other experiential and environmental factors, and so on?

These are important questions for those attempting to describe the process by which people make and modify singular moral judgments and for those concerned with influencing long-term patterns of moral choice. Findings such as those reported in the Greene (2004) study, combined with increasingly coherent accounts of the role of emotion and feeling in memory and learning (see Jensen, 2005 for an accessible synopsis), suggest that any pedagogically useful account of moral judgment and choice must take emotion and feeling into account.

This insight is by no means original. There is a long philosophical and popular tradition of understanding moral judgement as involving emotion and feeling. In particular, one 18th- and 19th-century tradition that provides some help in addressing questions such as these focused on the moral and emotional concept of "sensibility."

Though the philosophical and literary arguments that supported this earlier approach to the role of emotion in morality had severe shortcomings and suffered from considerable equivocation in their expression, I believe that these arguments, disinterred and reconstituted, can provide us with an approach to incorporating the stream of new physiological discoveries about moral choices into a fruitful set of theories about the nature of moral decision making. Such theories may, in turn, provide teachers with a starting point for effective moral instruction.

I will argue, here, that a key to understanding both how we make singular moral judgments and how we develop "character" (at least in one sense of that term) is understanding the role of "sensibility." What I mean by sensibility is, roughly, *a continuing and coherent set of emotions/feelings, sensitivities, dispositions, and priorities, which tend to both influence choice and provide a privileged set of premises in reflective decision making.*

I believe that our sensibilities help connect our emotions to our moral reasoning and to our moral choices; and through these, our sensibilities help us to develop our characters.

Sentiment in Moral Choice

What drives moral decision making, if not logical or material necessity? This question has two interpretations: that of asking for the causes of moral choice and that of asking for the source of premises in singular moral judgements. A large measure of the answer to both sorts of questions lies in the role of emotion and feelings in moral questions. The recent research previously described reflects a long interest in the role of emotion/feelings in moral judgement, some of which I will review.

Two 18th-century British philosophers, David Hume (1777/1965) and Adam Smith (1759/1976), made similar observations about the role of emotion and feeling in moral decision making. Hume (1777/1965) writes, "Reason judges either of matter of fact or of relations" (p. 126). But though reason, when fully assisted and improved, be sufficient to instruct us in the pernicious or useful tendency of qualities and actions; it is not alone sufficient to produce any moral blame or approbation. Utility is only a tendency to a certain end; and were the end totally indifferent to us, we should feel the same indifference towards the means. It is requisite a sentiment should here display itself, in order to give a preference to the useful above the pernicious tendency." (p. 125)

In other words, reason may apprise us of the facts of a situation, including the outcomes of certain choices. But only when we invest the situation and the choices with feelings are our preferences motivated.

Similarly, Smith (1776/1976) writes that "[r]eason may show that this object is the means of obtaining some other which is naturally either pleasing or displeasing. But nothing can be agreeable or disagreeable for its own sake, which is not rendered such by immediate sense and feeling" (p. 506).

These simple observations lead to many consequences, among which is Hume's (1776/1976) famous elaboration of the "no *ought* from *is*" position. We are not moved to action by facts alone. The prospect of emotions of pleasure or pain, or the arousal of certain feelings, must be added to the mix.

Moreover, Hume believed that what makes an action a moral good rather than merely utile, or beautiful, and so on, is, in the words of W.T. Jones (1969), first that "[i]t is a pleasure resulting from a consideration of character or motive"; and second "it is a disinterested approbation" (p. 342). Here, "character" refers to a person's inward life, motives, priorities, and so on. "Disinterested approbation" is a product of what Hume called an "internal sense or feeling which nature has made universal in the whole species" (as cited in Jones, p. 345). Hume's concept somewhat parallels modern developmental theories such as those on the growth of empathy, and he appears to have taken something of a developmental view of this internal sense, though he believed that it was inborn in all people. Further, he believed that our ability to form moral judgments grows from an initial state in which we only consider what affects us closely or what we're immediately acquainted with, toward a wider moral view, by means of empathetic consideration, in situations we don't know much about, of how an action affects those who are involved.

Senses of Sensibility in the 18th Century

These philosophical arguments both reflected and encouraged the interest of a host of popular writers in their examination of a concept seen as central to character, personality, and morality and based in emotion/feelings: that of "sensibility." But 18th-century popular versions of sensibility are of several sorts, some of them far removed from the construct I want to elaborate. Still, the contrasts and connections between these early popular versions and the one I want to discuss here should be useful. These earlier uses of the term included at least the following:

1. One sense of sensibility that runs through 18th-century literary discussion is described by Jean Hagstrum (1982) as "heightened emotional consciousness and quickness of feeling" (p. 9). In this version, one has sensibility to the extent that one is emotionally sensitive. We see this sensibility praised for its own sake in 18th-century British fiction, as in the title character of Richardson's *Pamela*, whose sensibility is outwardly apparent in her great delicacy (and also in her striking inability to remain conscious during confrontations). Leland Warren (1990) notes that the physiological notions of the day assumed that acuteness of feeling and imagination, and quick apprehension and understanding, were always inborn and thus not easily "teachable." Thus, one either had or lacked sensibility.

2. Another sense involves the tendency to judge one's choices solely by how they square with "the worthiness of one's feelings" (Warren, 1990, p. 34). Sensibility, here, is strong feeling used as argumentative authority and involves a spontaneous and "genuine" set of feelings about a given situation. Stephen Cox (1990) wrote, "The argument of sensibility may be very loosely defined as persuasive discourse that tends to equate intellectual authority with the power to display or elicit emotional susceptibility" (p. 64). While this version of "having sensibility" retained substantial support among both popular and philosophical writers, it was criticized as well. Hume, at one point, developed an argument that supports a positive view of this sort of sensibility, but the argument is equivocal. In *Enquiry Concerning the Human Understanding*, after observing correctly that moral praise or blame requires from us an element of approval or disapproval, Hume (1777/1965) concludes that

morality simply is the feeling excited by encountering situations and decisions: "The hypothesis which we embrace is plain. It maintains that morality is determined by sentiment. It defines virtue to be *whatever mental action or quality gives to a spectator the pleasing sentiment of approbation*, and vice the contrary" (p. 127).

Later, popular writers showed the practical problems with this sort of sensibility. Jane Austen (1811/1975) in *Sense and Sensibility*, for example, used the experiences of the young Marianne to show that judgement based entirely on a foundation of genuine feeling is suspect for several reasons: First, because the feeling may not be "genuine," but more importantly because feeling alone, without reason, self-control, and relation with others, will mislead and betray us. When Elinor, Marianne's sister, claims one of Marianne's actions lacks propriety Marianne retorts, "On the contrary, nothing can be stronger proof of [the propriety of the act], Elinor, for if there had been any real impropriety in what I did, I should have been sensible of it at the time, for we always know when we are acting wrong" (p. 61). Yet Marianne comes to regret this and other choices. Marianne's arguments of sensibility prove less effective than those of her sister, whose emotional sensitivities prove to be equally strong but tempered by reason.

3. A third 18th-century sense is one that privileges certain feelings. Walter Wright (1970) writes of Richardson that for him the hero of sensibility was one "whose impulses without being weakened had become the motivation of unselfish love" (p. 18). David Hume (1777/1965), without using the term "sensibility" to name what he wrote of, nevertheless postulated an ideal moral decision-maker as one who relies on a certain feeling "in order to give a preference to the useful above the pernicious tendencies" of the facts in a situation (p. 125). "This sentiment can be no other than a feeling for the happiness of mankind, and a resentment of their misery" (p. 125)

In more modern times, this advancement of certain feelings to the fore in moral decision making has often been a feature of psychological theory of morality, especially of cognitive developmental psychology. Piaget (1932/1997) and Kohlberg (1981) supposed that certain feelings tend to naturally and preferentially motivate and inform the moral choices of people at certain stages of development. Kohlberg went so far as to claim that true morality—its highest stage—involves a love of justice.

4. A fourth sense, one with a long tradition, sees sensibility as a praise-worthy, particular balance between feeling and reason, "the obedient passions . . . under the domination of reason," as Mary Wollstonecraft (2008/1788) put it in *Mary, A Fiction*. The particulars of this balance vary in 18th-century popular writing. Some versions of it look very much like "a routine notion of upright living" (Cox, 1990, p. 65) (i.e., sensibility as conformance to a socially approved set of priorities). Some particular balances seem to take a form that places sensibility in the same category as taste, cultivation, and discrimination—as a mark of being "classy" (see Raymond Williams, 1976, p. 236). Knightley, in Austen's *Emma* (1975 [1816]), embodies this sort of balance.

   This general sense of the term has many historical precedents and several famous descendants. Aristotle, who in his discussions of emotion in the *Rhetoric* and the *Nichomachean Ethics* anticipated modern approaches to understanding the nature of emotion, defined this balance as one with many dimensions. "Anyone can become angry," he writes in the *Ethics*, "[t]hat is easy. But to be angry with the right person, to the right degree, at the right time, for the right purpose, and in the right way—that is not easy" (Aristotle (2016), 1125b, pp. 32–33). Interestingly, this quote serves as an inscription for a very popular late 20th-century work, Daniel Goleman's (1995) *Emotional Intelligence*, which also advocates a particular sense of sensibility based on a balance very much in the tradition of Aristotle's *sophrosyne*. Goleman's balance includes "abilities such as being able to motivate oneself and persist in the face of frustration; to control impulses and delay gratification; to regulate one's moods and keep distress from swamping the ability to think; to empathize and to hope" (p. 34). On this reading, one may "have" sensibility to a degree, rather than either having it or not.

   Other 20th-century psychological writers have also developed versions of what we are calling an 18th-century notion of sensibility. Dewey's (1922/1957) balance between the demands of habit/impulse and the benefits of deliberation—what we tend to call (and praise) today reflective decision making—is very much in this tradition.

5. A final 18th-century version of sensibility is that of Immanuel Kant. Kant's (1781/2008) account in *The Critique of Pure Reason* described the necessary though unexaminable conditions of our consciousness

and our encounters with the world as our sensibilities. These operations of the mind are our organizing principles of reality, "categories" we live by, time and space, for example (Kant's own listing of categories in our sensibility hearkens back to Aristotle). Kant thought of our sensibility as universal and fixed, constituting our ability to encounter and interpret things in the world—and making it impossible for us to directly encounter "things in themselves," if they exist. Significantly, he called the workings of our sensibilities a "'transcendental aesthetic," an all-encompassing operating theory of the world around us. "All thought must, directly or indirectly, by way of certain characters, relate ultimately to intuition, and therefore with us to sensibility, because in no other way can an object be given to us" (Kant, 1781/2008). In Kant's use of the term, all members of our species not only "have" sensibility, but also share the same sensibility.

Eighteenth century uses for sensibility vary in important ways, but taken together they anticipate, to a degree, the sort of sensibility I will describe later in the chapter. These older concepts stress a connection between emotions/feelings on the one hand and rational decision making on the other. They also raise questions about the roles of inherited and experiential/instructional influences on moral judgement and choice. These issues are important ones for considering parents', educators', and communities' options in moral education.

[handwritten margin note: a lot connects from 18th C to now]

A Note on Emotion and Feeling

At this point, it is useful to point out that 18th-century conceptions of emotion and feeling were a bit different from late 20th- and early 21st-century neurophysiological conceptions. Alasdair MacIntyre (1965), in his introduction to a collection of Hume's moral works, complains that Hume "sees feelings, sentiments, and passion as given and unproblematic. We just have the feelings we have" (p. 16). But Hume does have a notion of a difference between emotions and feelings. Though he uses "sentiment" as a term covering both emotions and feelings, he speaks of many particular feelings, including "affection or disgust, esteem or contempt, approbation or blame" (Hume, 1965/1977, p. 128), and the complex attachment to mankind mentioned previously. But he also implies that feelings are based on something else: He speaks, as was mentioned earlier, of "the pleasing sentiment of approbation." This suggests that at least part of what motivates approbation is that something is pleasing, which in turn is what modern neuroscience identifies as one emotion.

In Hume's writing, there seems to be an assumption that a tendency toward certain feelings is a "natural" part of human psychology. He speaks of benevolence, in its various forms, as being a given of human nature, though it can be distorted by circumstances and habits.

Modern neuroscience, on the other hand, distinguishes between emotion and feeling on physiological and chemical grounds. Eric Jensen (2005), in summarizing research, says emotions are hardwired and "biologically automated" in the brain, though the chemical content of emotional response is present in other parts of the body. The emotions include "joy (pleasure), fear, surprise, disgust [which Hume saw as a feeling], anger, and sadness. Cross-cultural studies indicate that these six expressions are universal" (p. 73). The amygdala especially seems to be the brain-based center of emotion. "Removal of the amygdala is devastating. That destroys the capacities for creative play, imagination, key decision making, and the nuances of emotion that drive the arts, humor, imagination, love, music, and altruism" (p. 75)

Feelings, on the other hand are "our culturally and environmentally developed responses to circumstances. Examples include worry, anticipation, frustration, cynicism, and optimism" (p. 73). These, say researchers, work physiologically in a different way, involving the whole body rather than focused sections of the brain. Jensen presents, in capsule form, the roles of emotion and feelings in the decision-making process: "Experiences generate emotions—which generate thoughts, opinions—which generate the responses we call feelings—which strongly influence whether a student will be motivated to take action or not" (p. 78).

Here, feelings are hybrid concepts, with as much ideational composition as emotional. Though there is some difference, conceptually, in the 18th and 20th century accounts and different foci of study, it is not hard to see the similarities.

Features of Sensibility Explained

I would like to return to the conception of sensibility with which I began this chapter, as a notion somewhat paralleling the biological accounts discussed earlier, which includes a set of emotions/feelings, sensitivities, dispositions, and priorities, which tend to influence moral choice and provide a privileged set of premises in reflective decision making.

In the light of what has been discussed, several features of this account can more readily be explained. First, this concept differs from earlier versions of sensibility in being neutral about the emotional and rational content. That is, in the sense of the term I wish to discuss, everyone brings some sensibility to bear on moral choices and judgements. We are not lacking sensibility if we do not present some particular weighting of emotional and rational priorities. The question of what sort of sensibility is to be preferred is a separate question from that of whether one has sensibility. Everyone brings some sensibility to moral/ethical decisions, though we may bring differing sensibilities to such decisions.

Second, the earlier discussions help to provide details of the other features of my account of sensibility.

Disposition, to start, refers not only to recurring behavior, but to the origins and contexts of that recurrence. We may be *pre*disposed by our emotional temperaments (whether explained in terms of genetic inheritance and chemical balance or by the constraints of human nature and divine dispensation) and by our experiences and developing personalities to form, by way of emotional reactions to experiences, recurring feelings about similar situations. These, in turn, help account for recurring choices and conscious decision making on moral issues. And the habits of behavior we have developed through recurring choices work to move us to similar choices in the future.

Our emotions and feelings also make us susceptible or sensitive to certain elements in a situation. Even in popular 18th-century fiction, the "person of sensibility" (except perhaps in the sense of the term that focused *only* on emotional sensitivity) was selective in her or his emotional awareness, and it was this selectivity that helped to determine how the person of sensibility construed or framed the moral problem. Our sensibility is partly constituted by a tendency to notice certain features of a moral issue rather than others, as when we notice our own feelings or desires first, overlooking those of some other party in the situation.

Our sensibility includes the emotions and often complex feelings that our construal of an issue arouses. If I perceive real need in some person affected by my decision or choice, my temperament and habits may help to generate feelings of, say, compassion or pity. In ways that are suggested by the experiment described at the beginning of this chapter, these emotions and feelings, in turn, may either help motivate a choice of action or else help formulate key premises toward a singular moral judgement.

Sensibility includes priorities. These are tempered by the recurring progress, from experiences through choices I previously described, over a lifetime of problem solving (to use the Deweyan term for it). Fully or partly conscious, these priorities serve as privileged, "default" premises in reflective decision making. That is, our moral priorities tend to appear as important premises in moral arguments and, unless contravening considerations arise in a given decision, tend to tip the scales in favor of certain conclusions (see Cullity, 1994).

Finally, what I call "sensitivities" refers to the selection of perceptions that we actually attend to in any situation that calls for an ethical judgment. Rather than the heightened displays of emotion that 18th-century writers associated with sensibility, what I mean by sensitivities includes the "facts" of a situation that we notice and assign importance to, and the construction we give to those things to which we attend.

We never "see" everything about a given situation that calls for an ethical judgment. But what a given person attends to in such a situation both contributes to and is influenced by our dispositions and priorities. For that matter, if we are not sensitive, in a given situation, to another's possible harm, we will not characterize the situation as actually calling for an ethical judgment.

Some philosophers, including David Wiggins (2007), suppose that there are real "objects of value" that those within a given "moral community" are always sensitive to, and which provoke the emotional responses all members of that community have, to situations that call for moral or ethical judgments. Wiggins (2007) writes that "there is something in the object that is *made for* the sentiment it would occasion in a qualified judge, and it brings down the sentiment upon the object as so qualified" (p. 149, emphasis in original). He sees all value judgments, including moral ones, as having an objective existence that some are more expert than others in perceiving.

This attempt to see an objective existence of value in the world has the effect of turning value issues into empirical ones. My observations about the role of sensitivities in ethical sensibility certainly do not imply this. While it is likely true that in given "communities" of many sorts—geographical, cultural, occupational, and so on—people commonly attend to similar sets of facts in what they see as occasions for moral/ethical judgment, it is not necessary that they do so. It is likely that many factors and not just community membership play a role in determining the features of a situation to which an individual is sensitive. Because of this, to speak as we often do of categories of sensibilities (artistic sensibility, military sensibility, etc.) is, at best, a broad generalization that masks somewhat unique (and perhaps changeable) individual sensibilities.

As an answer to the question of from where, given the logic of value issues, our moral and ethical premises come, these features of the sensibility we always bring to such decisions provide important details. Our sensibility provides us with a selected set of emotions/feelings, facts, dispositions, and priorities that, whatever else may add to our consideration of an issue, can be counted on to matter to us personally in reaching a decision. As an answer to the question of what motivates moral or ethical choice and whether it is based in reflection, the features of our sensibility can be counted on to move us toward choice because they include the emotions and feelings that help constitute commitments.

Developing an Ethical Sensibility

From what sources do our sensibilities arise? Can they be deliberately developed or changed? Answers to these questions directly affect such issues as the possibility of moral education and the development of a professional ethic.

The 18th century was cautious in its hope for developing the sorts of sensibility its writers praised. As noted earlier, the physiological assumptions of the day had it that acuteness of feeling and imagination, quick apprehension, and understanding were always inborn. It followed that "[i]f sensibility depends largely on innate qualities, it is hardly surprising that even the boldest writer hesitates about claiming to teach it" (Warren, 1990, p. 32).

Nevertheless, despite this caution, and despite the significantly varying views of what constitutes sensibility, period writers noted other sources of a developing sensibility. Jane Austen's novels often turned thoughtfully to such matters. In *Sense and Sensibility*, Marianne, the sister of such acuteness of feeling and reliance on feeling alone to form judgement, is shockingly disappointed in love. Though the disappointment nearly kills her, it also works a sort of sea change in her sensibility (in my usage of the term), awakening her to the merits of a suitor she had earlier dismissed and helping her to develop new priorities for her life and choices. In this way, Austen reminds us that emotionally sharp experiences can be a source of change in our sensibility, making us sensitive to new phenomena, helping to establish new feelings in response to these phenomena, and bringing new considerations to the fore in moral judgments and choices.

Similarly, she traces the development of the sensibility of Emma Woodhouse in *Emma* (Austen, 1816/1975). Here, we find not only emotionally wrenching events working to change the heroine's default priorities, but also her constant interaction with a person she admires and her deliberate reflection on her choices and possibilities that cause her to modify her dispositions and find new ways to frame situations that require choice. James Boyd White (1984) writes that

> [t]hrough her "conversation," rational and playful with Knightley, Emma comes to reject her view of manners as artificial modes of behavior to be adopted as techniques of social success and to see them instead as the application of the whole intelligence to the meaning of what one says and does, to the nature of the relationships—the friendships—one establishes with others, and to the character one makes for oneself in the process. (p. 193)

Today, we have increasingly useful knowledge of the genetic and physiological processes that underlie a developing sensibility. We are also increasingly aware of how emotion is tied to learning and the integration of learning (Goleman, 2012; Ledoux, 1996; Pert, 1997, Zull, 2002). While we recognize the constraints of temperament and genetic inheritance generally, we also can reaffirm what Austen observed about the ways emotionally powerful experience, reflective decision-making, and interactive instruction can affect sensibility, and through sensibility our moral and ethical choices. Moreover, we are considerably more aware today of the role of socialization in forming and reforming our sensibilities (Arnstine, 1995). We are increasingly more knowledgeable about the webs of influence—from family and friends to work, sociocultural influences, and communities—that help to inform our priorities, focus our sensitivities, and form our dispositions (see Bronfenbrenner, 1979).

With these insights, it is possible to recognize that the long history of inquiry into moral and ethical decision making and action, fragmented though it is, has a common core. There may be many sources for our developing moral sensibilities, including the religious, cultural, and social environments we are emotionally attached to or strongly affected by; the principles of ethical behavior we forge for ourselves out of emotionally charged experience and imaginative projection; our genetic and developmental heritage; our reactions to received instruction; and, finally, our conscious, deliberate attempts to understand and reconsider both our moral choices and what has influenced them.

Sensibility in the Formation of Character

We are in a period of renewal of interest in education's role in developing character. Many scholars believe that our interest in educating for character arises whenever we believe ourselves to be in a period of rapid social change (McClellan, 1999, for example) and its attendant problems. Often, some writers maintain, a concern with educating for character conceals an agenda aimed at preserving or returning to "traditional" moral preferences and choices (McClellan, 1999) or traditional social practices and institutional functioning (Purpel, 1997). Individual character, it is then believed, is the foundation of social preservation.

McLellan (1999) provides an example: He says that at the beginning of the 20th century, American character educators, facing a period of changing economic and social conditions and the extended school attendance period that was a consequence of these changes, looked to create methods to help maintain traditional ideals of masculinity and femininity (in what was seen as a "feminized" school environment) while at the same time helping boys acquire the virtues necessary for success in business. Interscholastic athletics, for example, was a favorite of character educators because it purportedly helped adolescent boys learn virtues that differentiated them from girls—"individual excellence and the importance of team effort"—but also helped prepare them for excellence in a complex work world (p. 53). As schools changed focus to become more knowledge and skill oriented to reflect and assist in changes in the broader society, some educators looked for ways to retain traditional moral notions and to adapt them to new conditions.

If that is also the concern of today's character educators, then the effectiveness of their efforts depends first on overcoming several important though not new difficulties. The first problem is conceptual: Not only are there several very different senses of character in use among character educators today, but there is a tendency among such advocates to confuse one sense with another.

There is, first, a difference between an ideal sense of character and a descriptive sense. In the ideal sense, we do not speak of character at all unless we mean to speak of good character. Thus, we say that someone either does or doesn't "have character." We might compare this usage to that of one of the 18th-century versions of sensibility, in which a person of sensibility possessed certain admirable qualities and others did not.

But there are also several sorts of descriptive senses of the term. Character educators speak of character alternatively as the stable set of ordinary responses and behaviors to mundane moral situations, and as those moral responses and behaviors that are only displayed in situations of stress, difficulty, or unobserved choice. To illustrate the second of these, consider famous epigrams such as Lincoln's: "Nearly all men can stand adversity, but if you want to test a man's character, give him power"; or Macaulay's quip: "The measure of a man's real character is what he would do if he knew he would never be found out." At least the first of these descriptive senses is very much parallel to the version of sensibility I have put forward as a key to understanding how we make moral judgments. In this sense, it is appropriate to describe different types of character, with different emphases and priorities.

A final source of unclarity arises from uncertainty about whether, in speaking about character, we are speaking only about people's actual choices and behaviors or about rationale and/or commitments. Though there is considerable verbal attention to the latter formulation in the work of contemporary character educators, the actual programs put forward seem to focus almost entirely on the former. This is so much so that scholars such as Alan Lockwood (1997), after reviewing character education writings, concludes that "character education is construed as any effort to combat undesirable behavior" (p. 177) and the movement's emphasis on transmitting society's "core values" may be seen in almost entirely behavioral terms.

Even well-regarded writers about character education often fail to be clear about the sort of character they are most interested in educating. Both Thomas Lickona (1991) and Kevin Ryan and Karen Bohlin (1999), for example, explicitly define character in Aristotelian language that emphasizes reasons and commitments as well as "right" behavior. Ryan and Bohlin explicitly deny that character education is concerned with prescribing particular choices to moral problems. Though character itself is "an individual's pattern of behavior . . . his moral constitution" (p. 5), character education, they say, is "about developing virtues—good habits and dispositions that lead students to responsible and mature adulthoods" rather than what they term "right views" (p. 190). But their "Character Education Manifesto" is clear that character education should be concerned with instilling complexes of *behaviors* that constitute good habits and dispositions (e.g., self-discipline).

Lickona's (1991) account, more than Ryan and Bohlin's, gives only passing attention to "knowing the good and desiring the good (p. 51) and gives considerable attention to "doing the good." His considerable attention to implementing character education in schools focuses almost entirely on strategies for bringing about desired behaviors and habits.

What follows from the conceptual unclarity is the problem already implicit in the discussion: What do we attempt to educate when we educate for character? If character is those behaviors we exhibit under stress (or the reasons we rely on, or what we find ourselves cherishing in such situations), then our task is to prepare students for the worst. If character is an ideal set of behaviors, then we need to reach consensus on such an ideal, whether they are Aristotelian, some version of Christian, or another set, and we need to focus on helping people to display these.

What seems to be a necessary feature of all such programs, however, is the need to recognize the role of sensibility in pursuing them. While it is possible to directly elicit certain behaviors, it is not possible to directly move students to "see" moral decisions as including certain significant facts rather than others or to be sensitive to certain elements of a situation or another person's engagement in it. It is not possible to directly instill certain priorities that give precedence to some evidence over others in deciding what's right. It is problematic, at this point, to physiologically activate emotions and create complex feelings that help to motivate choice. If students' moral sensibilities are not addressed, character education amounts to behavioral conditioning. In short, to focus plans effectively for character education, there must be investigation into the possibility of educating sensibilities.

In light of this, moral education, seen as character education, the development of a professional ethic, or as any other form, is a complex matter. Our task includes acquiring the technical knowledge and skills needed to integrate the influences—physiological, developmental, and logical among them—on our own and our students' sensibilities. Just as importantly, it requires that we review and confirm our commitments and obligations—and surely these are emotionally constituted concepts—to our clients, our communities, and our ideals. In some areas, we have only a rudimentary knowledge of our task. In others, we have been reluctant to engage in full public discussion. Only in the light of these considerations will our knowledge of what constitutes moral and ethical decision making have an educative application. Then we may ask what manner of sensibility best serves those ends and may find an answer to this and other instrumental ethical questions that matter to us as educators.

CHAPTER FOUR

DEVELOPING A KINDNESS-ORIENTED TEACHING ETHIC

What Is a Kindness-Oriented Teaching Ethic?
Why Prefer It as a Teaching Ethic?

THE PREVIOUS CHAPTERS HAVE attempted to clarify the notion of kindness and explain how our ethical judgments are typically determined by our ethical sensibilities. It remains to make clear how to describe a teaching ethic consisting of an ethical sensibility that is oriented toward kindness.

An ethical sensibility is a continuing and coherent set of emotions/feelings, sensitivities, dispositions, and priorities that typically influence both ethical arguments and ethical choices. Kind actions are recognizable as ones that (a) demonstrate certain relational features of the one acting kindly (K) and the receiver of that action (R), as well as others affected by K's action that show K in a position to mitigate R's need in the context of the act's effects on others; (b) demonstrate K's belief that R's need should be mitigated and that K should attempt to mitigate it in a context in which K's action is voluntary and discretionary; and (c) demonstrates R's relevant knowledge and skill in successfully mitigating R's need.

It follows that a kindness-oriented ethical sensibility would involve (a) a continuing sensitivity to some other's need; (b) emotions/feelings in response to that need that may, variously, be ones of determination to help, have compassion, and/or have empathy; (c) a disposition to take action to mitigate the other's need with regard to the welfare of others affected by K's actions; and (d) a reasoned priority of doing so. Further, for such a sensibility to result in actions that are recognizable as kind, the one acting must have and deploy relevant knowledge and skill needed to mitigate the need.

Such a sensibility would act as a kind of default in situations requiring ethical decisions. It would not guarantee acts of kindness in response to client needs, and defaults are overcome by special circumstances—including circumstances that may, for educators, justify caring actions or decisions based in a desire for justice. But a teaching ethic that is oriented toward kindness is one that will result in a tendency to decide and attempt to act kindly in responding to clients' needs.

It remains, however, to be argued whether such a teaching ethic, based in a kindness-oriented ethical sensibility, is to be preferred over competitors. There are a number of approaches to defending a kindness-oriented teaching ethic that are worth considering. For instance, we should consider the merits of and problems with competitors in relation to those of a kindness-oriented teaching ethic (KOTE).

Why a Kindness-Oriented Teaching Ethic?

My descriptions of both a KOTE versus a teaching ethic oriented toward caring or toward justice of these orientations will be limited to focus on those features that I want to highlight. The need on certain occasions and for particular ongoing teacher-client relationships for either caring or for justice in teachers' ethical decision making is, of course, clear; but there are features of both that create ethical problems that, in my view, make a teaching ethic oriented toward kindness a superior one.

Caring involves an ongoing relationship between the one caring and the one cared for. For however long such a relationship continues, it is, in important ways, exclusive. That is, to be in a caring relationship, the one caring must work to not only understand but also to adopt the motivations and desires of the one cared for (Noddings, 1984). To act kindly, in contrast, K must understand and respect R's needs rather than R's motivations and desires and consider R's needs *in the context of those of K him- or herself and of those who may be affected by an attempt to mitigate R's need*. A teacher acts in the context of a caring relationship primarily or exclusively with regard to the one cared for, leaving the effects of caring acts on others affected by such acts mostly or entirely out of consideration. Moreover, teachers act in an environment that includes a range of clients—many students, parents, colleagues, and citizens—so that a tendency to focus, overall and in the long run, on relationships with many individual clients may not even be feasible for teachers. Caring relationships with individual clients are sometimes needed but pose some problems as the basis for a coherent teaching ethic.

Consider, as an example, a situation in which a student—Mike—is continually late for a first-period class. He has accumulated both warnings and in-school suspensions. Ms. Smith, the first-period teacher, fearing that Mike is on the road to quitting school, embarks on a project to keep this from happening. She welcomes Mike into class when he is late, adopting Mike's view that he does try to get to school on time but works a late shift and shouldn't be sanctioned if he oversleeps. Smith goes out of her way to spend time in class bringing Mike up to date on what he has missed that day, and she defends Mike in faculty and administrative discussions of his status. She also covers for him so that the administration doesn't discover his tardiness. Mike is gratified and grateful and does try his best to get to first period on time. Other class members, however, are angry with Ms. Smith, believing her actions to be favoritism. Others complain about the time Ms. Smith spends on Mike alone rather than with the class as a whole or with other individual students.

Here, Ms. Smith is establishing a caring relationship with Mike. This benefits Mike as a student and a person. But this comes at a cost to others in the class and to the personal and academic welfare of the class (and, perhaps, to Mike, given the class's reaction to his relationship with the teacher). While that outcome may not occur, it can be a real problem when it does.

Justice may well demand that Ms. Smith follow school rules and keep (what I will later call) "professional distance" from Mike; but, again, at what cost to Mike? While enforcing a rule here is "fair" in the context of treating Mike as others would expect to be treated, Mike's particular needs are ignored and perhaps exacerbated. Moreover, in either scenario, the teacher herself risks damage to her effectiveness with her class.

We might envision a sort of teaching ethic continuum that, at one extreme, focuses mostly or entirely on the welfare of a given individual client, and at the other extreme on the welfare of an entire group and of individuals' relationship to that welfare. In this image, a caring-oriented teaching ethic is at one extreme and a justice-oriented teaching ethic is at the other. Justice, in its various forms, is always concerned with how the welfare of a given individual or smaller group, in particular contexts, affects or is affected by the welfare of the larger group or members of that group. The notion of justice as fairness (Rawls, 1971) captures, in part, this orientation.

 A KOTE, on the other hand, occupies, on this continuum, a middle ground, and one that, in general, better serves the welfare of an educator's clients than either of the other two orientations for these reasons: First, an educator, especially one working in a school, is almost always working in a context that requires him or her to focus primarily on the educational and personal welfare of individuals, but in an environment in which the educator's efforts in that cause may affect or be affected by the welfare of other clients. And those clients, in both singular ethical judgments and for ethical decision making generally by educators, may extend from the classroom ultimately to the community and larger society. Therefore, a teaching ethic that focuses primarily on individual welfare, but in the context of groups affected by an ethical judgment, as a default orientation serves best both individual students and the larger community.

In contrast to both a caring and a justice orientation, common wisdom among educators has, for generations, included advice that represents itself as a call to "professionalism" in the form of a different ethical stance: a call to establish a professional distance from one's students.

I received advice when I was a novice teacher to develop a professional distance from my students and other clients. I confess that I never fully understood that concept, but I gathered at the time that it embodied an argument for a relationship with students, parents, and other clients (but with students especially) that featured a somewhat friendly but generally reserved classroom demeanor, a willingness to take on all student or parent academic concerns while politely refusing to take on their personal or interpersonal problems, a concern for by-the-book fair dealing with students, coupled with a general withdrawal from engaging in what are seen as supererogatory activities of kindness or personal caring and the maintenance of an undefined but purportedly admired attitude of wise detachment.

More formally, scholars have variously defined professional distance as "selectively withholding expression of personal values in professional life, whether the values are embodied in emotions, preferences, relationships, conduct, or ideals" and the difference between a professional's power and a client's vulnerability (Martin, 1997, p. 84) . This last point especially puts the focus on the relationship—social and ethical—between teachers and students. It reminds us of what Paulo Freire (1970/2005) noted: that the wrong "distance between the teacher and the taught" works against any life-changing student learning.

There are benefits to teachers and students in that distance: the ability to "kidwatch" in ways that lay the groundwork for effective instruction of individual students; emotional distance also helps teachers deal with the large "relationship load" that can overwhelm them otherwise. It can also elicit respect from students and other clients by suggesting control; and it may encourage student autonomy.

But professional distance, whether social or emotional, has drawbacks, too. In effect, professional distance emphasizes the needs of the teacher above the needs of individual and groups of students (and other clients). By rejecting decision making that addresses clients' personal welfare to address only their academic and other needs that make up teachers' "professional" objectives, professional distance as a default approach to teaching relationships ignores, among other things, a large and growing body of research that demonstrates the role of social-emotional learning in acquiring academic learning. Related to this point, professional distance serves to create a classroom environment in which relations between teacher and student, and among students, minimize only the features that researchers associate with "authoritative" parenting and teaching—features that are again highly correlated with student success in many senses.

A KOTE conforms to what developmental research has found to be an optimal parenting or teaching style. Building on the early research of Diane Baumrind (1971) and Maccoby and Martin (1983), researchers have found that parents whose default approach to parenting is what researchers call "authoritative" tend most often to have children who, in many ways, are most successful in school and in life. Other styles found by researchers— authoritarian, permissive and uninvolved—are less associated with these outcomes and more associated with undesirable outcomes such as failure in school, problems with the law, and more.

The features that together constitute these styles, features that researchers now see as a context that moderates the influence of specific parenting practices on the child (Darling & Steinberg, 1993), include level of parental warmth, level of responsiveness, level and kind of control, and level and kind of communication. Each of these features, and their lack, has been independently found to be strongly associated with children's success or failure in both school and non-school settings; and certain combinations of these features are what constitute the four styles of parenting. Independently, high levels of warmth—affection, positive responses, and so on—are associated with more secure attachment, higher self-esteem, more empathy, more altruism, higher IQ, doing well in school, less aggression, and less delinquency. Low levels of warmth, on the other hand, are correlated with more suicidal thoughts and other mental health issues, declining school performance, and greater risk of delinquency.

High levels of responsiveness—picking up a child's signals and reacting sensitively to a child's needs—are associated with early language acquisition, higher IQ, rapid cognitive development, secure attachment, more social competence, and more compliance with adults. With control, high levels of consistency in rules and procedure, reasonably high expectations for behavior, and quick, nonemotional, and appropriate punishment are associated with general competence, high confidence, and low risk of delinquency. Finally, high levels of open, two-way communication between child and parent are strongly correlated with a child's emotional and social maturity and more success at friendship.

Authoritative parenting style is one in which there are high levels of warmth and responsiveness; clear, reasonably high expectations for the child that are well monitored; and lots of two-way communication between child and parent. This general mode of parenting is strongly correlated with a child's high self-reliance, social competence, good grades, less psychological distress and misconduct, less drug use, and less delinquency. While these outcomes vary to some extent given cultural factors, the sex of parents, and parental beliefs and goals (Chao, 2001; Smetana, 2018), the research has provided a strong basis for preferring this parenting style. Authoritarian style, which tends to feature a one-way communication, permissive style that is lacking in control, and uninvolved style, which is weak in all four areas, tend to produce problems. More children growing up in authoritarian homes than for those in authoritative homes are either passive or defiant in school. More children in permissive homes than in authoritative homes have slightly lower grades, display more aggressiveness, and display immature behavior with peers. Children whose parents or caregivers display an uninvolved style are, in comparison to those with authoritative parents, more likely to show insecure attachment, show impulsive and antisocial behavior, have a low orientation to achievement, engage in more delinquent behavior, and be involved in early sexual activity.

For schools and for teachers, the lessons seem clear. Schools and classrooms need to establish a relationship with students that mirrors an authoritative style of parenting (i.e., a relationship that establishes an environment of high warmth and responsiveness, high and reasonable expectations for both performance and personal comportment that are well monitored, and constant two-way communication). Given that children spend increasing amounts of their waking life, as they grow to adolescence, in school and school activities, schools and classrooms provide either a continuation of or an alternative to the relationships established at home. For those children who experience an authoritative parenting style, it is important to their continuing success that schools and classrooms mirror that style—call it "management style," "teaching style," or something similar. For the minority of children growing up with non-authoritative parenting styles, it is crucial that schools and classrooms provide a clear authoritative alternative that helps mitigate problems that otherwise may have a greater likelihood of occurring.

The connections of a kindness-oriented teaching ethic for educators to the research on parenting styles are important to note. In teachers' ethical decisions that concern students' school and personal welfare, we consider as kind those ethical decisions that stem from positive and accurate recognition of a student's situation and needs, often recognized through two-way communication with the student, carried out with intent to mitigate problem situations, and within guidelines that acknowledge others affected by the decision—especially when we recognize the decision's successful outcome. While teaching styles of any of the four varieties described leaves room for kind actions and practices, an authoritative style seems most likely to produce and be produced by means of a kindness-oriented teaching ethic.

A teaching ethic of kindness serves to further students' social-emotional learning (SEL). A growing body of research supports the view that SEL is crucial to not only students' future success in life, but also and more immediately, their success in learning.

SEL aims at so-called "soft" learning outcomes directly. Johnson and Johnson (2004) define SEL in complex terms:

Social and emotional learning may be defined as the a) mastery and appropriate use of interpersonal and small-group skills (e.g. recognizing, managing, and appropriately expressing one's emotions), and b) internalization of pro-social attitudes and values needed to achieve goals, solve problems, become emotionally involved in learning and work, and succeed in school and throughout life. (p. 30)

As the definition notes, SEL's focus is on abilities that are viewed as instrumental to learning that is academic, but also learning that leads to success beyond academics and beyond schooling. Toward academic success, Joseph Zins and colleagues (2004) summarize research on SEL that describes school attitudes, school behaviors, and school performance factors—they list 39 of all these—that are both constitutive of school success and associated with SEL abilities. Attitudes include more academic motivation, the ability to cope effectively with stressors, positive attitudes toward school, and more. Behaviors include fewer absences, more class participation, a lower rate of conduct problems, greater effort to achieve, higher engagement, and other features. Performance features include doing better in various subjects, increases in performance over time, better problem-solving and planning abilities, use of higher-level reasoning strategies, higher achievement test scores and grades, and more.

Success beyond academics and beyond schooling has many possible meanings, and SEL research associates many of these as ultimate outcomes of SEL. Advocates argue, for instance, that SEL can create skills in negotiation and conflict resolution that improve chances of success in work and in the community; enhance individuals' sense of belonging and self-confidence that, in turn, make for happier individuals (Johnson & Johnson, 2004); and even help create peace and lessen conflict between people—as one fifth grader is reported to have figured, people "wouldn't get mad at each other [a]nd they'd treat each other a lot better" (Sung, 2018).

It is not hard to see how a teaching ethic that is oriented toward kindness fits an emphasis on social and emotional learning. If teachers approach their relationship with students, consistently aware of students' needs, those who are affected by teacher actions, and the needs of the teachers themselves; if they are motivated to take action (and, in so doing, model taking action) to mitigate students' needs; if they are skillful and knowledgeable in their actions so that student needs are consistently met—in other words, if they are acting kindly in their professional life—then they are contributing in the ethical domain to students' acquisition of SEL abilities. And if SEL abilities are indeed keys to academic, personal, and communal success, then a kindness-oriented teaching ethic is important to that success as well.

I will also argue that what's good for students is good for teachers; the methods and goals of SEL for children may well turn out to be successful methods and goals for developing teachers with a kindness-oriented teaching ethic.

One interesting finding concerning teachers' use of SEL practices bears on the argument I will make in the last chapter of this book. In a study by R.J. Collie and colleagues (2011), the researchers found that "[t]eachers' SEL practices are . . . positively associated with their commitment to the profession" (p. 1048). That is, it may be either that the value teachers place on SEL practices that attend to student life and relationship abilities has something to do with teachers' recognition of the broader value of education and their work in it or the reverse (i.e., the value teachers see in their work has something to do with their concern for students acquiring SEL abilities—perhaps as contributing to the overall good teachers who are committed to furthering for individuals or community). I will argue in the final chapter that a KOTE is consistent with and may contribute to a commitment to an idealized aim for teaching.

A KOTE is consistent with what students actually say they want from teachers. In a long-running effort to discover a satisfactory answer to the question of what students want from their teachers, I have asked my university classes over several decades and at several institutions to brainstorm a list of features of "the ideal teacher." While my sample has been fairly large—an average of 50 students per semester for at least 20 years, I make no claims that the effort followed even quasi-experimental procedures, nor that my sample has been representative of all students of all ages. Still, the effort has produced fairly consistent results. In describing the results that follow, note the role that relationships, and especially relationships that feature elements of teacher kindness, have played in my students' experiences and hopes.

1. My method has been to ask first for students' input on particular features of what they see as an "ideal teacher." Then I ask the students to

find categories of features in the list they have, together, constructed. My students over the years, at both public and private universities at which I have taught, have answered my question "What are the features of your ideal teacher?" with surprisingly consistent categories of features, though phrased in varying forms. They have categorized their features in the following ways:

a. Social/relational abilities, personality traits, professional abilities, commitments, and ethical traits

b. Interpersonal relations features, knowledge/skills in teaching, personality features, motivation and purpose traits, management skills, professional and personal ethics, a well-rounded life, and personal/professional "style"

c. Personality features, intellectual abilities, ethical traits, professional and workplace abilities, social skills, emotional dispositions

d. Personal traits, academic and professional abilities, relationship skills, attitudes and commitments toward teaching and learning

2. Using form "d"—one of the most common formulations—here is how these categories have been unpacked:

a. Personal traits: Ethical traits, personality features, emotional proclivities, and lifestyle features

b. Academic/professional abilities: Intellectual strengths, professional and subject-matter knowledge, teaching and management skills, and workplace skills

c. Relationship skills: Interpersonal abilities and teaching "style"

d. Attitudes and commitments: Attitudes toward the subject matter, toward the value of teaching, and the goals, ideals, and strength of commitments to these

3. Specific likes under these have tended to include the following (note the underlined features):

a. Under attitudes and commitments: Having a passion for subject and for teaching, having high expectations and being persistent in them, having interests outside of school, being active in the life of the school, <u>being able to make learning purposeful to students, working to bring out students' potential, honoring student achievement, viewing teaching as a vocation rather than a job</u>

b. Under personality traits: Open-minded, creative, having a sense of humor, having a positive life outlook, being adaptable, confident, willing to admit mistakes, punctual, dependable, clean, appropriate, <u>approachable</u>, trustworthy, honorable, modest, mature, brave, self-disciplined, energetic, <u>empathetic, kind, caring, compassionate</u>

c. Under academic/professional abilities (partial list): <u>Varies methods to meet student needs; adjusts to new students and circumstances; is encouraging to each student</u>; knows subjects deeply; <u>motivates</u>; is a clear, persuasive, skilled speaker; <u>maintains a safe and comfortable environment for learning; doesn't give up on students; is respectful of students; is supportive of student interests; makes learning purposeful</u>; is organized, prepared, patient, and collegial; navigates school systems well

d. Under relationship skills: <u>Is caring</u>, <u>approachable</u>, authoritative, patient, and <u>fair</u>; <u>respects students and differences; has personal relationships with each student</u>; communicates well; is <u>empathetic and understanding</u>; has sense of humor; is modest; is <u>perceptive of student situations</u>; is <u>interested in students' lives</u>; is good with parents; is <u>able to consider multiple perspectives</u>; <u>acts ethically in professional and personal life</u>

It is striking that students in many classes, over many years, and in different parts of the country have tended to stress the underlined features, and how closely those features, taken as a group, suggest the features of teacher kindness. Who, after all, is in a better position to recognize the features of teachers' behavior that correlate with student well-being in school than students themselves?

A KOTE may play an important role in bringing about a new consensus on the long-term and ideal aims of education for our society. Finally, I will argue in the last chapter of this book that, as a society, our long-term survival and prosperity may depend on reaching for and achieving a long-term consensus on our societal and educational aims/ideals. I argue that a teaching ethic that is oriented toward kindness has a role to play in working toward both a consensus on all this and on a particular direction of that consensus.

How Can We Help Teachers Develop a Kindness-Oriented Teaching Ethic?

An ethical sensibility that focuses on kindness is constituted by sensitivities to others' needs; feelings of respect, empathy, or compassion for those needs; dispositions to respond to those needs; and priority given to those responses. The success of the acts that are consequences of that sensibility—necessary to recognizing such acts as kind ones—depends in large measure on the person having that ethical sensibility also having the knowledge and skills required to mitigate others' needs. If we are convinced that such a sensibility is to be preferred in our teachers, how can we bring that about on a large scale?

One approach, of course, is to make it a policy to seek out and employ those men and women who already demonstrate such a sensibility and demonstrate it as a KOTE. This could be accomplished by prescreening applicants using any number of existing or specially developed instruments or observational techniques and by careful observation of teaching candidates in both simulated and actual field experiences, together with feedback from students and from the candidates themselves.

But, as is the case for most of what we come to recognize as desirable features in teachers, we can't always expect to attract to teaching enough candidates who already possess a kindness-oriented ethical sensibility. Moreover, a campaign to further KOTE in classrooms must also address working teachers. How can we help to develop more teachers with a kindness-oriented teaching ethic?

There are a number of approaches worth considering, especially in combination.

The first is to *take advantage of recent research into the physiological bases of ethical choice*. The research of Joshua Greene and his associates (2001) has been especially instructive, as noted in an earlier chapter. To repeat: Greene and his colleagues' original "Trolley" experiment and its results are now well known:

A runaway trolley is headed for five people who will be killed if it proceeds on its present course. The only way to save them is to hit a switch that will turn the trolley onto an alternate set of tracks where it will kill one person instead of five. Ought you to turn the trolley in order to save five people at the expense of one? Most people say yes. Now consider a similar problem, the footbridge dilemma. As before, a trolley threatens to kill five people. You are standing next to a large stranger on a foot bridge that spans the tracks, in between the oncoming trolley and the five people. In this scenario, the only way to save the five people is to push this stranger off the bridge, onto the tracks below. He will die if you do this, but his body will stop the trolley from reaching the others. Ought you to save the five others by pushing this stranger to his death? Most people say no (p. 2105).

An important take-away from that original research is the distinction between "impersonal" and "personal" moral judgments. Greene and colleagues observed that when subjects were asked to make moral judgments for others they responded with moral reasoning; but when they were asked to see themselves in similar situations, they responded first with the emotions that the situation elicited from them. Paxton, Unger, & Greene (2012), in subsequent research, found that different portions of the brain were activated in impersonal and personal moral judgments. Indeed, impersonal moral judgments look the same in the brain as non-moral value judgments. Further, the research revealed that, in many personal moral judgments, there is conflicting activation in brain areas associated with both cognitive reasoning and with emotional response. This occurs in situations where there are "difficult" personal moral dilemmas in which utilitarian values require "personal moral violations" (Greene, 2004, p. 389). Greene defines these violations as ME HURT YOU responses that contemplate actions that are likely to cause severe harm to particular persons for whom the actor is directly responsible. Importantly, Greene also discovered that in these difficult moral dilemmas the brain areas activated tended to favor cognitive judgments over emotional response.

In later research, Paxton, Ungar, and Greene (2012) showed that inducing people to make counter-intuitive moral judgments, or at least to consider them, is possible. They gave the cognitive reflections test (showing people non-moral counter-intuitive truths) before giving moral dilemmas, and this resulted in less emotional/intuitive and more moral utilitarian judgments. They also showed that well-designed arguments and more deliberation time influenced more utilitarian judgments. They concluded that (a) "reflection can influence moral judgment when people are induced to distrust their immediate intuitive responses"; and (b) that strong argument is more persuasive in modifying intuitive emotional moral judgment, but only when people have extended time to reflect on the argument (pp. 175–176).

It may be that, using this and similar research as a guide, teacher educators can develop both discussion-based and experience-based tools to stimulate teacher reflection that first stimulates an emotional, "personal" response that leads to recognition of situations that call for ethical judgment—a necessary first step toward the factual inquiry into client problems and the self-reflection that may lead to a response of kind choice and action. That, indeed, is the task, as I discussed in an earlier chapter, my colleague and I found was called for in working with the teachers who failed to see the situations in a casebook of ethical issues as actually being ethical issues. While those who are labeled as sociopaths seem constitutionally unable to recognize and respond to the distress of others, we are all less sensitive in this way than we are capable of becoming. Indeed, research indicates that we all vary in the extent to which we are even consciously aware of our internal physiological states—our "interoceptive awareness" (Garfinkel & Critchley, 2013). The more aware one is, the more intense one's emotional experience. This finding points us toward a need to encourage current and future teachers and for them to pay special attention to both the needs of others and their own emotional responses to those needs. In this way, a greater sensitivity to such needs is more likely to become part of educators' decision making.

Next, this research suggests the need for teachers and educators to develop or take advantage of situations that they first respond to with emotion. It seems that while there are culturally based emotional responses to personal ethical judgments, such conditioned responses are not universal (though sensibility theorists sometimes suppose that there are indeed universally emotion-provoking situations (see Wiggins, 2007). Deliberately creating or practically making use of what teachers respond to as requiring real, "personal" ethical judgments and then guiding teachers toward reflective examination of the situations can develop habits that lead to kind, ethical decisions. We should note that this general approach is not new; John Dewey, for instance, in works such as *Human Nature and Conduct* (1922/1957) and *How We Think* (1933) pointed to the need to think more productively by getting past an initial response of falling back on habits and instincts, whether or not they are emotional ones. The value of the research of Greene and others is both in uncovering physiological origins of the problem and opening up thinking toward practical approaches to overcoming it.

A second approach to developing a KOTE in teachers is one that we may see as also important for working with practicing teachers in the approach previously described: *Make use of skilled coaches*. For preservice teachers, trained teacher educators should oversee field experiences and carefully structured simulations that challenge students' emotional responses to others' possible harm. Developmental research has long noted that altruism in children is causally linked to role-taking ability (see Shaffer, 2005). Children who receive training in role-taking skills afterward show more pro-social behavior (Chalmers & Townsend, 1990). The same should apply to teachers and teacher candidates.

Pro-social reasoning and sympathetic and empathic reaction to others' distress is also linked to pro-social behavior (Shaffer & Kipp, 2014). It would seem likely that skilled coaching in these areas would also be effective in working with adults. "Skilled" is the key word, here; we don't currently require teacher educators and in-service supervisors to develop the expertise needed for this. Moreover, effective coaching requires equality, teacher choice, respect for teacher voices, joint reflection, dialogue, praxis (application of new skills), and reciprocity of learning for teachers and coaches. Jim Knight (2011) calls this a partnership approach to teaching; and all these features seem to require both a recognition of needs by both parties and coaches' ability to address those needs, with attention to possible consequences to others. In short, it would seem that effective coaching for KOTE is best accomplished by coaches with both an understanding of methods that provoke a kindness-oriented reasoned response in those they coach and a KOTE themselves.

Another approach is to *apply what we are learning about the importance of students' social-emotional learning (SEL) to teachers and preservice teachers*. SEL foci for students tend to include identifying emotion, perspective taking, self-control, interpersonal problem solving, and conflict resolution (Taylor, Oberle, Durlak, & Weissberg, 2017. All these goals are ones that, applied to teachers, are relevant to a kindness-oriented teaching ethic. Kimberly Schonert-Reichel (2017) notes that "[w]hen teachers are trained in the behavioral and emotional factors that influence teaching and learning in the classroom, they feel better equipped to prepare and implement classroom management strategies that deter students' aggressive behaviors and promote a positive learning climate" (p. 138). And it is no accident that successful classroom management practices strongly resemble what I described as authoritative teaching style, which, in turn, is compatible with a KOTE. It should be noted that successful programs preparing teachers for SEL once again depend heavily on well-trained coaching staff, not only for the development of formal instruction, but also for modeling and for both participation in and facilitation of informal learning.

Another approach is to *adopt teaching, administrative, and technological practices that make it easier for teachers and preservice teachers to deploy a kindness-oriented teaching ethic.* For example, one teaching practice adopted by an increasing number of teachers, especially in the case of teachers of younger children, is one-on-one meeting time (see Stinnet, 2018). Meeting briefly and regularly with students to discuss a range of academic and personal issues can give teachers insight into student problems and needs and provide teachers with deep knowledge of their students' life situations that will help teachers both mitigate student problems and needs and develop actions that will minimize harm to other students affected by their actions—key elements of a KOTE.

A number of teaching methodologies regularly place students in situations that result in those students facing "personal" moral dilemmas. Problem-based learning (PBL), notably, often results in students, in real contexts, facing these challenges. When preservice teachers are learning to construct useful PBL curricula, and when practicing teachers construct actual plans for PBL, they need to be prepared for the inevitable moral choices students are called on to make in such arenas. Training teachers in PBL, then, is an opportunity to help them consider the multiple needs of those students working together to make their plans and the needs of those affected when students try to put their plans into action. A KOTE is needed in such contexts, and teachers should be helped to see the value of this teaching ethic for such situations. In fact, the more teachers turn to PBL in their classrooms, the more they will, of necessity, adopt a priority for addressing their students' needs in responding to personal moral challenges.

Similarly, cooperative education methods create dilemmas for students working out ways to deal with personal moral issues that inevitably arise when equitable and effective ways of working toward group goals are required. Teachers approaching these dilemmas with a KOTE are better equipped to help their students with these needs, and this too argues for teacher preparation that focuses as much on teaching ethic as on other aspects of curricular effectiveness.

The current interest among educators in "mindfulness" practices for their students also offers opportunities for teachers to increase their awareness of and sensitivity to what is happening in students' lives in the classroom. Mindfulness focuses on self-awareness and awareness of those people and situations around us, and so provides both students and teachers with the basis for multiple perspectives on the consequences of their possible and actual choices (see Flook, Goldberg, Pinger, & Davidson, 2015; Sung, 2018).

One administrative example of practices that would make a KOTE possible and effective is looping—having one teacher for a class of students over two or more school years. This arrangement makes effective relationships between teacher and students more likely by once again laying the groundwork for teachers acquiring more knowledge of students and student needs. Some research notes the connection between looped classrooms and benefits such as higher student test scores (Hill & Jones, cited in Barshay, 2018; Battistich, Schnaps, & Wilson, 2004; Birch & Ladd, 1997), which would not be surprising, given that students respond to strong relationships with their teachers by increased involvement with school and academic participation.

An example of technological innovation with the potential for helping teachers and preservice teachers develop a KOTE is virtual reality. Parsons & Mitchell (2002) found that "[v]irtual reality technology may be an ideal tool for allowing participants to practice behaviors in role-play situations, whilst also providing a safe environment for rule learning and repetition of tasks" (p. 430). Current reliance on games, simulations, and feedback on actual classroom behaviors is useful but limited. Virtual reality greatly expands possibilities for structured situations and more fully natural targeted responses. One example of this potential, a medical training model using virtual reality (VR) called virtual standardized patient training (Hubal, Kizakevich, Guinn, Merino, & West, 2000), uses a combination of VR and pedagogical instruction to create situations that were formerly and expensively simulated by trained actors; the settings being ones used for patient-practitioner dialogue and patient-interview training. In the hands of trained coaches and instructors, VR focusing on student or other client interactions with teachers would offer opportunities for ethical decisions by teachers, which would approximate "personal" ethical choices and so provide a basis for training that could lead to teachers developing a KOTE.

This chapter has been concerned with identifying a kindness-oriented teaching ethic, arguments for preferring such an ethic as the default approach to teacher ethical decision making, and some possible approaches—separately or in concert—to helping new and established teachers acquire a KOTE. Previous chapters have attempted to clarify the notion of kindness and its role in singular ethical judgments and in the pattern of sensibility that underlies our general approach to such judgments; it can also serve to form a KOTE. It remains to view teacher kindness in a larger context, that of educational ideals and the ultimate purposes for education and for teaching. That concern I will take up in the final chapter of this text.

CHAPTER FIVE

KINDNESS AND THE DEMOCRATIC IDEAL

KINDNESS, AS I ARGUED earlier, implies knowledge of the situation and of the needs of the recipient of one's actions—whether or not R is aware of or able to articulate that situation and need (though for R to see the act as kind, R must be aware of the need). But a kind act is not limited to addressing an R's current situation and needs. We may act kindly with the longer-term needs of R in mind. Thus, a teacher may decide to recommend a student for an advanced course, recognizing that the student may not take the initiative to apply herself for a course that the teacher knows will take advantage of the student's talents and perhaps even raise her chances for admission to a good college. Such an act may turn out to be a kind one, even though the student may not feel a need for it; though she may recognize such a need at some point in the future. This concern for the future welfare of a given student, a group of students, or all students our work as teachers will ultimately affect underlies the issues raised in this chapter.

The Problems With Acting in Support of Students' Long-Term Needs

While a concern for acting in ways that address students' future needs is an admirable one, as teachers, the certainty with which we may "know" the future situations and needs of our students diminishes, in most cases, the further into the future we project. Still, teachers do and sometimes feel they must attempt to act kindly toward a student or students by projecting to a future near or far in which the teacher's actions may affect their welfare. Not only in situations such as this, but also in teachers' visions of students' adult opportunities and challenges are such actions formulated. At an even further distance—chronologically but also conceptually—are teachers' visions of students' situations in what their society and their world could at best or at worst become.

As I noted earlier, my students' image of an ideal teacher has generally included the feature that such a teacher is "committed to teaching." When we speak of teachers having a "commitment" to teaching, among the things implied by this attribution is that teachers see some long-term or overall value to teaching that provides purpose to their work and warrants their continued participation in the occupation.

If teachers' commitment to the profession leads them to explicitly consider, as they sometimes (though perhaps rarely) do, the direction that education, broadly speaking, should take to bring about an ideal future for their students, they must then consider what actions to take toward or with their students to work toward that ideal.

Whether it *should* be within a teacher's purview to consider these educational ideals and students' needs as part of working toward them I will consider shortly. But even the mention of educational ideals as a part of a KOTE provokes questions about some obvious problems with such a view. Let us consider a few of these problems.

Do teachers and students "need" an educational ideal? To act kindly, K must recognize in R a need. For R to recognize K's action as kind, R must also recognize that he or she has a need. One plausible account of what we, in general, mean by a need is "an imbalance, lack of adjustment, or gap between the present situation or status quo and a new or changed set of conditions assumed to be more desirable" (Leagans, 1964). But in this account we may see an ambiguity between a need as something empirically or logically necessary or sufficient for bringing about any given state of affairs, and, on the other hand, a need as something necessary or sufficient specifically to improve someone's welfare. This is the difference between, remarking, say, that "cleaning fluid is needed to remove those marks from the whiteboard" and saying that "Harry needs to be closer to the whiteboard, since he has trouble seeing what's written on it; and, as such, is at a disadvantage." It is primarily with these second "welfare" needs that we are concerned, here.

We have needs of the second sort in areas of our lives that are economic, social, aesthetic, moral, or spiritual, among others. Psychologists such as Maslow, Frager, and Fadiman (1970) have spoken of needs in terms of physical, social, and psychological requirements for happiness and achievement. Moreover, it is recognized that such needs may be "felt" or "unfelt." These observations suggest several problems.

First is the practical problem of determining when a felt or unfelt need is an actual need. Very often, a person's view or feeling that something is needed for his or her welfare either is incorrect or is confused with a mere desire for that situation to occur. And, also very often, unfelt needs are eventually though not immediately felt as needs by the recipient of a kind act. But an educational ideal not only is positioned in some perhaps unknowable future so that it is not apparent when it may be "needed"; but such an ideal, by its very nature, is difficult to fully articulate, so it is usually not entirely clear what we may come to have a felt need *for*.

Second, not all needs directly concern a "present situation." A given K, as illustrated at the start of this chapter, may correctly anticipate a welfare need in some R that will arise or be felt in the future but "needs" (in the general sense of being required) to be addressed in the present. The problem for K is correctly predicting the future welfare need and how to address it.

But to say that students in general "need" to become aware of, accept the ultimate value of, and work toward arriving at some educational ideal complicates the matter further. To say this is to claim both a present and future welfare and a general need: Students must acquire now a felt welfare need to work toward such an ideal to work toward a future they and/or their society will need to achieve to survive or prosper. The present need must become a felt one to motivate students toward the need that extends into the future.

Finally, it is not entirely the case to say that the need students have to work toward an idealized future is only the students' problem. Teachers making this claim imply a need on their part as committed to that ideal. And this "hidden" need leads to a second problem category for the view that a teacher acting toward students with a commitment to an educational ideal in mind can be acting kindly, as part of a kindness-oriented teaching ethic. After all, a teacher acting with the dominant motivation of self-benefit is not acting kindly.

Kindness, coercion, or paternalism in teaching for an ideal. It is tempting to claim that a teacher who acts, toward students, in a way that addresses his or her own view of what is best for students' future welfare is at best acting paternalistically and at worst coercively. Can we still be acting kindly toward our students, individually and as a group, with an eye to the part our students will play in the long-term, idealized aims that we as educators have for education? While on its face this notion appears to substitute teachers' values, desires, and needs for those of their students, a closer look suggests that educators, to justify the work they do with and for their clients, *must* both possess and connect their professional actions to long-term educational aims and ideals.

We begin by observing that educators do not serve their students' immediate, much less their longer-term, learning and personal needs if what they do in school is purposeless. As Neil Postman (1996) argued in *The End of Education*, teachers and students must have, and if possible share, a narrative that connects their current situation to longer-term and even idealized goals that give their current and future educational activities an ultimate meaning.

Purpose may be seen in shorter-term goals associated with a day's studies or a school year's studies, and also in intermediate goals that connect these studies with tangible future outcomes such as doing well in higher levels of education or acquiring a desirable job. But the aims that, in the broadest sense, anchor the work that teachers and students do are also the ultimate justification of individual educational acts, where these are seen as part of an ongoing narrative. That narrative gives overall meaning, coherence, and direction to what students do and what their teachers do for them.

One way of understanding this hierarchy of purposes is to consider the notion of "educational progress." Progress implies a goal toward which activity is directed and assessed, with the possibility of markers of success along the way. It is generally possible to assess our progress toward short-term and intermediate goals if we can first become clear about how we will recognize the achievement of such goals and if we can develop formative and summative assessments that address those criteria. It is more difficult to assess progress toward those aims we will call "ideals," since these are inherently unattainable in full or are at best "moving targets." But there still may be ways to mark progress in the direction of those ideals. That, after all, is what educational standards should be, given a conception of what they mark progress toward. But standards without an ideal in mind are ultimately indefensible and arbitrary, as would be any assessment that is not connected to some purpose. That is one reason teachers, students, and others affected by educational choices and actions need an educational ideal.

To the extent that both teachers and students are mindful that teaching and learning acts are ultimately connected to progress toward educational ideals that both students and teachers value, what teachers do serves students' needs, teachers' needs, and—given community-wide buy in—the needs of the broader community. So, a teacher may act kindly in working toward an educational ideal with students, even if the need of the one acting, as well as that of the recipient(s), is also served—so long as R's need is dominant. Note the role played by consensus concerning educational ideals in such a scenario. For a teacher to be recognized as acting kindly here, recipients must undergo a process of discussion and consensus toward becoming aware of a need. This, in recent decades, has been notable in this country by its absence, and these decades have been marked by many false starts and arbitrary reversals in American educational policies and programs.

Interestingly, from this perspective teachers must be recognized as acting *un*kindly toward their students—both individually and as a group—if their teaching is not anchored in not only short-term and intermediate goals, but also in an educational ideal. For without that anchor, what teachers do ignores students' ultimate educational needs for purpose in their education. In the introduction to this book I mentioned the "teaching sentence" I asked beginning education students to complete. This argument is evidence that teachers at all levels should recognize that the completion of that sentence must include a clause that reads "for these immediate, longer-term, and ideal aims."

Given this, both problems raised are dealt with. Students do, in fact, need an educational ideal, though this need must be a felt one to motivate students to work toward such an ideal and to assess the learning offered them and their progress through that learning, toward that ideal. And teachers' commitment to an educational ideal is not paternalistic or coercive if students become aware of and accepting of that ideal as a need.

The Kindness-Oriented Teaching Ethic and Educational Ideals

Given a need for an educational ideal, what ideals exist from which to choose? In the United States, with the exception of recent decades, we have traditionally associated schooling with what we have viewed as certain valuable, even idealized aims. In teacher preparation programs, beginning with the earliest public normal schools of the 19th century and persisting to

nearly our time, teacher candidates had been urged to adopt long-term, idealized aims for their work, aims that were to guide their work over a career.
Indeed, many normal schools and their higher education descendants maintained an atmosphere reminiscent of a religious revival meeting (though the
Protestant church flavor eventually became muted; see Tyack, 1967 for a
useful account). Of late, though, such injunctions have often been more lip
service than a basis for real service to teachers in their work. At the very
least, teachers have traditionally believed that their real work involves more
than complex technical activity, and that it involves something to do with
the welfare of children and communities.

One product of the concern that teachers' behavior should be consistent
with long-term aims has been the many constructions of "codes of ethics"
and other legal or quasi-legal documents outlining teachers' accountability
to their various publics. But recently, as part of a renewed interest among
philosophers of education in the focus of professional ethics I have labeled
here as a "teaching ethic," philosophers have tied arguments for teaching ethics to working toward particular idealized educational aims. Various visions
of a desirable society and/or society's members have given birth to various
conceptions of a teaching ethic founded on the need to address those visions.

Implicit in this tendency to tie the teaching ethic to idealized educational
aims is the assumption that a teaching ethic can be both consistent with and
contribute to addressing those aims. This point, in fact, is what I want to
argue for, here, with a particular educational aim in mind as a preferred
example. I will argue in this section that the most justifiable teaching ethic
to adopt for purposes of teaching in and enriching American democracy is
one based in kindness.

Americans hold to a variety of educational ideals. Some of these are
legacies of debates long past; some have their origins in the problems and
opportunities facing individuals and the nation at the moment. Too often,
however, Americans are unwilling to articulate clearly, even to themselves,
let alone publicly debate, the assumptions and hopes they carry with them
about the ideal ends of educating. Americans' views of what teachers should
strive for are often only implicit and sometimes contradictory. They generally consist of a number of prioritized or situation-based ideals—also unarticulated. This state of affairs makes it difficult to formulate broadly popular
educational plans and policies since Americans' commitments to long-term
educational aims generally only come to the surface when individuals find

something to complain about in the direction of current school policies and activities. On any given issue, there will be a body of citizens who find that given proposals take education "in the wrong direction." This in turn creates a great deal of equivocation and question begging, given our fondness for developing standards for schools and teachers to meet. Standards, as noted earlier, however clearly described and objectively measured, are likely to be unsatisfying tools for organizing teaching if they are without an anchor in the aims—what Donald Arnstine (1995) calls the "ideals"—that such standards are instrumental in addressing. Arnstine (1995) notes that "[i]deals are what people strive for. Standards are what they try to meet. You can fail to achieve an ideal, yet not be a failure. But falling short of a standard is what we *mean* by 'failure'" (p. 22). Our basis for seeing failure in American schools is in the unarticulated and usually unexamined connections between standards and the ideals they might address.

Standards, in short, are the mile markers we may reach along the way to a distant, perhaps unreachable (but well-loved) destination. This situation bears a striking resemblance to the fabled Xeno's paradox, in which a traveler who must, logically, travel half way to her destination as part of traveling the entire way there can, logically, never arrive—since wherever the traveler is, she must still travel half way to the destination first.

However, the point of having an ideal in mind is not to get there, but to move purposefully in that direction. In fact, an ideal provides the very description of a direction for our activities. Educational ideals stand in contrast to the usual sequence of outcomes educators associate with their teaching. Lesson objectives, intermediate learning goals associated with units and courses, and even the outcomes teachers work toward over years are ones we may achieve or fail to achieve (or rather our students may or may not achieve, at least in part with our help). Ideals are otherwise: They are, by definition, either unreachable or subject to constantly shifting descriptors. Whether we could actually observe their achievement if they were subject to completion is also an interesting question. Nevertheless, when we have ideals, we have stars by which to guide our travels.

It seems of little use to hold teachers and schools accountable to standards, then, without broad agreement about the ultimate purposes such standards may be argued to serve. Without such a connection of standards to ideals, the standards are ultimately unmotivated, arbitrary, unjustified, and/or unfair. They are mile markers to no particular destination, interesting only to travelers who, for reasons ranging from coercion or material incentives to idiosyncratic ambition, strive to reach them.

There are a number of persistent, though again often implicit, ideals that seem today to drive the several sorts of educational "reform" appearing in American public discussion. Some of these have origins in antiquity, and tracing their provenance and connections to American experience is an interesting exercise, though it is not one I will attempt here. Others are of more recent origins or still in the process of forming in public consciousness. Though writers have offered various descriptions, here is what I hope will be a useful account.

American Educational Ideals

Make an American citizen angry about some actual or proposed educational decision and he or she is likely to raise a rant against that decision that includes an objection to the direction in which that decision takes us. But if you were to press the issue with this angry citizen by asking for details about his or her view of the right direction for education, chances are the answer would come either in the form of shorter-term objectives or in a stumbling reference to an educational ideal that the dissenter can barely articulate. The fact is that today, except when our gut reaction to an educational proposal leads us to think a bit about why we don't like some decision in education, we Americans just aren't practiced in speaking about educational ideals. We aren't even very self-aware, as a rule, about the assumptions we carry around with us about the ideal aims of education. We are not mindful of our ideal educational commitments.

This is not surprising, since public discussion about outcomes at that level is quite rare, and there seems to be little thought by legislators, educational administrators, or even by teachers to develop community-wide conversations and consensus about what ultimately should justify our concern with educating—at least on a level much more sweeping than the immediate economic benefit education purportedly can produce.

Nevertheless, these gut reactions that schools are going in the wrong direction imply that we do indeed hold to certain educational ideals, even if they are tacit or unexamined. Moreover, I believe that most of us hold to a number of such ideals at once, without conscious self-contradiction, but also without much conscious prioritization. Without claiming to be exhaustive in developing it, here is a list of those ideal ends to which many

Americans—including American teachers—have made a commitment, however unarticulated and unexamined such a commitment may be, and the role education is to play in working toward those ideals.

1. A "materialist" argument for an educational ideal is one that, in my experience, most Americans find very attractive. Indeed, it seems to have been the dominant ideal in American thinking during the one period in American educational history in which there was explicit discussion of educational ideals and the means of addressing them: the long common school era. In this materialist argument, we conclude that the ideal of educating is to bring individuals and community to material success in the world. Such an end in view is an ever-shifting one because our view of material success changes as individual and societal conditions change. Indeed, the support for this conclusion generally comes in the view that many things in the world are in a constant state of change, and unless individuals and communities keep up awareness of the nature of those changes, they will not prosper in them or even survive. Education should be the way people and societies can find out how conditions are changing and what to do about adapting to the changes. Some versions of this argument focus on individual material success and some on what it takes for our society to compete, prosper, and dominate in such a changing world.

2. A "perennialist" view of an ideal aim for education focuses on fully developing the human potential, both individually and communally. Rather than aiming for material accumulation, the perennialist aim is for better people. The support for such an ideal is that, first, human beings, like every other species, have a certain unique potential as part of their special nature. Just as an acorn, under certain optimal conditions, can realize more of its inherited potential as an oak tree than under less good conditions, so human beings, properly raised and in optimal conditions, can become more fully what human beings have a potential to become. Conditions in the world may change, but what constitutes human potential is constant (though there have been and are various views of that potential's features). Education is then the one means by which the mass of humanity can be set on the road to perfecting itself.

3. Where the first two ideal ends of educating include a focus on society,

the **"existentialist" ideal** argues for individual autonomy, agency, and freedom. In this vision, every child will grow to be master of his or her own life, creating that life out of his or her own hopes and imagination, though recognizing that such a life, to be successful, must be lived in relationship with others. This ideal is supported with the observation that, though human potential may be constant, human construction of the world, human choices, and human hopes and desires are varied and, in combination, unique to each individual. For addressing this ideal, education must offer each individual both grounding and special opportunities for following a unique personal path.

4. In contrast, a **"reconstructionist" ideal** for educating envisions a perfect society (though the details of such a vision often vary. One common version popular in the West today is that of a "truly" democratic, egalitarian society). Such an ideal often arises from observing the imperfections of current society and recognizing that education offers both the opportunity for generations of people to learn how to create a better society and the chance to practice living in such a society in an education setting before applying that expertise in the larger world.

5. One final American educational ideal is the **"progressive" ideal** of the able individual problem-solver, who is at the same time the competent and willing steward of an existing democratic society. In this ideal, education is necessary to help individuals develop their expertise in thinking through and acting on the continual stream of concerns, opportunities, hopes, and fears of daily life while at the same time dealing with the problems of community life that can make or break individuals' chances of following successfully their own course of decision making. In working to preserve and extend the democratic community, individuals increase access to the information and connections they need to make good individual choices. Education is the key to effectively combining these two projects, through learning that revolves around problem solving, both by the individual and the community.

The first four of these ideals, and versions of their supporting premises, are as old as Western civilization, at the least. Sparta advocated a harsh version of the first, Aristotle championed the second, the Renaissance reinvigorated the third, and utopian visions older than Plato's have always been with us to motivate the fourth. Only the progressive ideal, perhaps, is uniquely American and of comparatively recent origin.

Are there any emerging educational ideals? One that is perhaps in the process of articulation, though it is not a uniquely American vision, is that of the ideal education being one that provides stewardship of the Earth by means of the knowledge, skills, and dispositions formed through generations of educating individuals toward that stewardship.

At any rate, it is crucial to observe that most Americans would approve of not just one but of all these ideal aims of educating, were they to be articulated clearly. We don't object to any of these per se. But we do prioritize them, though not usually in a fully conscious, coherent, and consistent manner.

And that is a real problem, not only for educators, but also for our society. Efforts at educational reform, much like efforts to address educational standards, ultimately are arbitrary without reference to long-term, even ideal aims. Reform implies desirable change *from* some state of affairs *to* some better state of affairs. But most if not all our society's debate has been focused on the "from" side of the vision, with very little aside from short-term objectives or references to competitive advantages on international tests, instead substituting for wide consensus about ideal aims of educating.

However, no widespread consensus about educational ideals is likely when there is no widespread public discussion of the alternatives. And we can't have such a discussion if our current commitments to educational ideals remain largely implicit and unarticulated. Among the ideals we seem to carry around with us, which should gain precedence?

It is sometimes possible to recognize, in the arguments for a teaching ethic that are put forward, the assumption of (though usually not an explicit argument for) the precedence of some educational ideal. For example, the care ethic that writers influenced, by the work of Nel Noddings (1984, 2005), and have advocated for educators seems to assume a radical existentialist ideal for teaching. In its insistence on "engrossment" with and "motivational displacement" to the desires of the one cared for, the care ethic's concern is focused strongly on the welfare of single individuals to the exclusion of either the welfare of those who may be affected by caring activities or the welfare of any larger community. If teachers' and students' activities are to be guided by any educational ideal that considers the welfare of these groups to be important, a professional ethic of caring won't do. Still, here, at least is a more or less explicit argument for a narrative to guide our actions in educating. If we are to work toward a greater consensus on an educational ideal to focus education, we need more such arguments, especially ones that attempt to merge some of the ambitions of the several ideals we seem to implicitly embrace.

Educating for Democracy

Among the several sorts of educational aims implicit in arguments over the direction of educational reform, one educational ideal at least arguably encompasses most of the range of hopes for education expressed by thoughtful Americans today. John Dewey's progressive ideal of education for the preservation and improvement of democracy articulates what seem to be the main hopes of a diverse group of thinkers: the concern for individual welfare by care-ethicists and other existentialists; the hopes for perfecting human nature of perennialist humanists and communitarians; the commitment to perfecting society that motivates reconstructionists; as well as the concerns for survival, prosperity, and dominance of those materialists whose concern is with increasing their nation's influence among the nations of the world and the material success of their nation's people. Add to these the priority of educating for critical thinking that at least seems to be a common thread among all these visions.

Dewey's (1916/1966, 1922/1957, 1927/1969, 1933) arguments for the ideal of a continuing democratic society contain elements and versions of all these and in that way point to a possible path for achieving a high level of consensus among advocates for education should real public discussion of educational ideals occur. However, Dewey's elaboration of that ideal provides, in some ways, an ideal distinct from the others.

Certain features of Dewey's notion of a democratic society and democratic living have been particularly influential in formulating an ideal toward which educators might strive. These include an ability and willingness of individuals to deliberate systematically on personal concerns, opportunities, and goals as well as issues affecting the community (Dewey, 1922/1957, 1933); a tendency in the larger society to increase "points of shared common interests" using recognition of those shared interests as "a factor in social control" and a "freer interaction between social groups"; open access to information and resources needed to make informed and useful decisions about matters affecting society; and constant adjustment of society's functioning to meet "the new situations produced by varied intercourse"

(Dewey, 1916/1966, pp. 86–88).

Also important to Dewey's conception is the sense of the contingent nature of the existence of a democratic society. There is nothing necessary about the appearance or the continuation of a democracy in his sense of that term. In the case of the United States, democratic living has been brought about, in part, as an effect of the development of science and technology under certain economic, geographic, and political conditions. Keeping democracy, increasing and improving it, requires real effort and constant education:

> A society which is mobile, which is full of channels for the distribution of a change occurring anywhere, must see to it that its members are educated to personal initiative and adaptability. Otherwise, they will be overwhelmed by the changes in which they are caught and whose significance or connections they do not perceive. The result will be a confusion in which a few will appropriate to themselves the results of the blind and externally directed activities of others. (Dewey, 1916/1966, p. 88)

He contrasted this vision with his picture of the "tribal" society, one that is static, exclusive, and insular—in ideas, knowledge, and loyalties, and sometimes in the physical sense—and sees nonmembers as outsiders or even enemies. The marked tendency of American society today toward tribalism provides a case study of the contingency and fragility of democratic living that Dewey observed.

Dewey's vision for the continuing maintenance and renewal of a democratic society depends in large measure on how much its individual members are aware of what's going on around them, how sensitive they are to the consequences of changing conditions, how effectively they make use of individual and shared experience, and how much they are capable of and disposed to make decisions, with others, concerning their own and society's welfare.

From this perspective, Dewey saw moral life as decision making involved with the overlapping interests and interactions of people with one another. In its widest sense, "[a]s a matter of fact, morals are as broad as acts which concern our relationships with others" (Dewey, 1916/1966, p. 357). Though, as he noted on several occasions, many of our decisions are habitual or impulsive, and moral judgments must usually be a result of thinking of a deliberative process in uncertain situations. Because every moral context is in some ways unique, each presents us with a problem on which to reflect, rather than a routine situation to be dealt with through our habits without thought.

In the progressive view, democratic life is interactive and seeking always to expand both individual initiative and general welfare. Dewey's (1927/1969) preference for education curricula that emphasize activity-based lessons is based in this aim for democratic skills. In *The School and Society* (Dewey, 1927/1969) he observes that in such classrooms, "Helping others, instead of being a form of charity which impoverishes the recipient, is simply an aid in setting free the powers and furthering the impulse of the one helped" (p. 16). Democratic moral life, Dewey believed, is, in situations involving our interaction with others, one that seeks to increase the capabilities of those involved in that interaction—their knowledge, skills, sensitivities, dispositions and defensible priorities, and their ability to mesh their individual ambitions and the welfare of the community—and to expand the bases of their common interests. To recognize democratic living, it seems, it is often less important to see all agreed on a given policy than to see all skillfully and willingly engaging in joint, deliberative problem solving in situations affecting all concerned.

Teaching in and for a democratic society, then, is indeed an essentially moral enterprise. If such a society is what we envision, strive toward, seek to maintain, and improve through our teaching, we must carefully choose, among other educational decisions, a teaching ethic that will best help us in that longest-term aim.

Kindness and Democracy

If teachers wish to model and to teach the sensitivities, dispositions, priorities, and skills needed to promote democratic interaction in society, they require a teaching ethic that leads them to consider their relation to individual and groups of students as part of a triad of interests in decisions that involve their relations with clients (both recognized and self-chosen). They must be concerned first with the welfare of the student or students with whom they are in a given instance engaged; they must consider their own interests in the matter at hand; and they must regard the interests of others whose welfare may be affected by actions they may take.

Most of all, teachers should keep in mind that their position as teacher significantly identifies the form of their ongoing relationship with their students. Most of their engagements and encounters with students are influenced by their commitment to seeing to students' welfare (including in that notion of welfare the task of increasing their competence in living in a democratic society, if teachers hold to that ideal). That, I argued earlier, is implicit in recognizing themselves as teachers. This feature of the relationships gives emphasis to one side of the ethical triad: that of the welfare of the student or students with whom teachers are at some moment and recurrently engaged.

What teachers need, then, is a teaching ethic that disposes them, in ethical decisions of teaching, to consider the welfare of students in the context of teachers' own interests and those of others who may be significantly affected by the decisions they make. A teaching ethic based in kindness has a number of features that directly address that need. And a teacher-student relationship that finds teachers regularly acting kindly with regard to student needs that are academic, personal, and social, by its very nature models qualities crucial to students recognizing and developing knowledge, skills, sensitivities, dispositions, and priorities that will enable them to function well in a democratic environment—and at the same time help create the sense of immediacy that research has associated with increased student engagement in the classroom. Consider the following:

1. The knowledge features of kind acts imply teacher insight into a student's or students' condition and context, coupled with the academic, personal, or social knowledge and skills required to help with student needs. Continued display of such knowledge and skills provides students with a model of abilities required to recognize and knowledgably contribute to the problems of others and of society. Exposure to a teacher's triadic concerns in acting provides a model for student consideration, not only of their own positions on public problems, but also of the need to reach out to consider the perspectives of and consequences for others affected by whatever public decision is chosen.

2. The intentional features of acting kindly imply the acknowledgement and valuing, even if not the approval of the views, perspectives, and needs of others in public discussions of public problems, and the intent to work collaboratively to address others' views along with one's own.

When students, in turn, recognize and value the respect teachers show them in addressing their needs, they can learn to display the same respect for the needs of others. The disposition to help when there is need can be developed, in part, through experiencing that help when it is needed.

3. The relational features of kind acts emphasize the connections between and among individuals and groups—the interconnectedness that stems from the consequences of particular acts directed by one toward another. Dewey (1927/1954) noted that "[t]he idea [of democracy] remains barren and empty save as it is incarnated in human relationships" (p. 143). Dewey's contemporary and acknowledged influence, T.V. Smith (1926), went so far as to argue that democratic living must involve extending the relationships formed in the family—the kinship that gives kindness, etymologically, its name—to what he saw ideally as a world-wide democracy, a "brotherhood of man" (p. 30).

4. The habits absorbed by students in a classroom whose relationships are founded in kindness are likely to be applied toward effective democratic relationships elsewhere.

In general, all the features of acting kindly address what Dewey described as the key features of democratic living. In acting kindly in response to students' needs, teachers increase points of shared common interests through their demonstrated interest in students' needs. Kindness in the classroom breaks down differences among students and student groups and encourages thoughtful consideration of other students' circumstances in acting toward any of them—a factor in self-regulation as social control. Kind action as the norm promotes informed decision making and emphasizes the need for sharing key information in decision making. And kind action models for students the unique and ever-changing circumstances that contribute to the needs of individuals and groups.

Finally, the contribution of a teaching ethic of kindness to democratic living comes from the establishment, in a classroom or school, of a feeling of mutual closeness—a recognition that we are all in this together, no matter our individual situations. This is the emotional environment that researchers generally call "immediacy" (Burroughs, 2007; Frymier 1993). A teaching ethic that emphasizes kindness results in actions that students see as lessening the distance between teacher and student but also among students themselves since the circumstances of the class or the school (and sometimes other affected clients) are always a consideration in the ethical actions of teachers. Research, especially in communications-related areas, has consistently shown a positive connection between a student perception of immediacy in the classroom and increased compliance with and engagement in the academic demands of the classroom.

Extend that feeling of immediacy into the larger community, as may well occur in generations of students growing up in an environment of kindness, and an important condition for valuing and pursuing democratic living will have been established and, we may hope, maintained.

So, a teaching ethic based in a sensibility of kindness, of the sort I have described, seems to me to be the best fit for promoting the ideal of maintaining and extending democratic functioning in society. Given the arguments of previous chapters about the nature of kindness and what constitutes the sensibility of kindness that provides a background to kind actions, the connection should be apparent. First, a KOTE requires attention to and skill in recognizing and addressing multiple perspectives in deliberating on actions that address client needs. Successful democratic living also requires honoring multiple perspectives in deliberating on problems affecting oneself and others. A teaching ethic of kindness is a complex and constantly self-adjusting cognitive and emotional framework for approaching ethical decision making. Democratic living demands this.

Moreover, a KOTE must, of necessity, be guided by assumptions about and commitments to what will address both the immediate and long-term welfare of those affected by educators' decisions. This must bring to light those assumptions and commitments, allowing educators and their students to examine their worth. In this way, ideals such as the progressive one may be examined and evaluated. Democratic living requires bringing to light and constantly assessing both individual and societal aims to work toward agreement on how to progress toward those aims and solve problems that arise in that effort.

When a teacher models a sensibility of kindness, students have a better chance of recognizing its elements, seeing its effects on their own welfare, and coming to value it in their own and fellow students' lives. Thus, they may work to acquire in their own lives the sensitivities, feelings, dispositions, and priorities that constitute such a sensibility for themselves, along with the thirst for knowledge and skills necessary to successfully act kindly.

All these features are also necessary to developing the able personal and public decision making that is the basis for personal success and democratic living. If, in the public discussion of ideals I believe to be necessary to a coherent and consistent approach to educating and to a teaching ethic, Americans should come to commit, as I have, to prioritizing education for democratic living, I believe they will embrace a kindness-oriented teaching ethic as instrumental to approaching that ideal.

In this chapter, I have attempted to make a case for idealized aims for educating as essential to a teaching ethic. In this book, I have tried to make a case for kindness as the central focus for teaching relationships with students and others who make up teachers' clientele. I hope that, at the least, these efforts will provoke thoughtful reconsideration of the immediate and ultimate value of teachers and what they do.

REFERENCES

Aristotle. (2016). *Nicomachean ethics.* W.D. Ross, Trans. Digireads.com Publishing.

Arnstine, D. (1995). *Democracy and arts of schooling.* Albany, NY: State University of New York Press.

Atwood, M. (1837). *The progressive reader or juvenile monitor.* Montpelier, VT, George W. Hill.

Austen, J. (1975 [1816]). *Emma.* London: The Folio Society.

Austen, J. (1975 [1811]). *Sense and Sensibility.* London, The Folio Society.

Baldwin, J., & Bender, I. C. (1901). *The expressive third reader.* New York, NY: American Book Co.

Barshay, J. (2018, May 21). Two studies point to the power of teacher-student relationships to boost learning. *Hechinger Report.* Available from http://hechingerreport.org/two-studies-point-to-the-power-of-teacher-student-relationships-to-boost-learning/.

Battistich, V., Schnaps, E. & Wilson, N. (2004, March). Effects of an elementary school intervention on students' "connectedness" to school and social adjustment during middle school. *Journal of Primary Prevention, 24*(3), 243–262.

Baumrind, D. (1971). Current patterns of parental authority. *Developmental Psychology Monographs, 4*(1, Part 2), 1–103.

Bellah, R. N., Madsen, R., Sullivan, W. M., Swidler, A., & Tipton, S. M. (1985). *Habits of the heart: Individualism and commitment in American life.* Berkeley, CA: University of California Press.

Birch, S. H., & Ladd, G. W. (1997, March). The teacher-child relationship and children's early school adjustment. *Journal of School Psychology, 35*(1), 61–79.

Bronfenbrenner, U. (1979). *The ecology of human development*. Cambridge, MA: Harvard University Press.

Burroughs, N. F. (2007, August 28). A reinvestigation of the relationship of teacher non-verbal immediacy and student compliance-resistance with learning. *Communication Education, 56*(4), 453–475.

Cameron, D., Inzlicht, M., & Cunningham, W. A. (2015, July 12). *New York Times*, p. 12.

Campbell, L. J. (1884). *The new Franklin fifth reader*. New York, NY: Taintor Brothers, & Co.

Campbell, L. J. (1886). *The new Franklin third reader*. New York, NY: Sheldon and Company.

Chalmers, J. B., & Townsend, M. A. R. (1990). The effects of training inn social perspective-taking on socially maladjusted girls. *Child Development, 61*(1), 178–190.

Chao, R. K. (2001). Extending research on the consequences of parenting style for Chinese Americans and European Americans. *Child Development, 72*(6), 1832–1843.

Collie, R. J., Shapka, J. D., & Perry, N. E. (2011). Predicting teacher commitment: The impact of school climate and social-emotional learning. *Psychology in the Schools, 48*(10), 1034–1048.

Cox, S. (1990). Sensibility as argument. In Conger, S. M., (Ed.), *Sensibility in transformation: Creative resistance to sentiment from the Augustans to the romantics: Essays in honor of Jean H. Hagstrum* (pp. 63–84), Cranberry, NJ: Associated University Presses.

Cullity, G. (1994, October). International aid and the scope of kindness. *Ethics, 105*(1), 99–127.

Cyr, E.M. (1901). *Cyr's fourth reader*. Boston, Ginn & Company.

Darling, N., & Steinberg, L. (1993). Parenting style as a context: An interpretive model. *Psychological Bulletin, 113*(3), 487–496.

Demarest, A. J., & Van Sickle, W. M. (1900). *The new education reader, book two.* New York, NY: American Book Co.

Demarest, A. J., & Van Sickle, W. M. (1901). *The new education reader, book four.* New York, NY: American Book Co.

Dewey J. (1916/1966). *Democracy and education.* New York, NY: Free Press.

Dewey, J. (1922/1957). *Human nature and conduct.* New York, NY: The Modern Library.

Dewey, J. (1927/1954). *The public and its problems.* Chicago, IL: Swallow Press.

Dewey, J. (1927/1969). *The school and society.* Chicago, IL: Phoenix Books.

Dewey, J. (1933). *How we think: A restatement of the relation of reflective thinking to the educative process.* Chicago, IL: Henry Regnery Company.

Dworkin, G. (1972). Paternalism. *The Monist, 56*(1), 64–84.

Eisenberg, N., Fabes. & Spinrad, T.L. (2006). *Prosocial development.* In W. Damon and R.M. Learner (Series eds.), & N. Eisenberg (Vol. Ed.), *Handbook of child psychology*, Vol.3, *Social, emotional, and personality development* (6th ed.), pp. 646-717. New York: Wiley.

Elson, R.M. (1964). *Guardians of tradition: American schoolbooks of the nineteenth century.* Lincoln, University of Nebraska Press.

Fichtenau, H. (1991). *Living in the tenth century: Mentalities and social order.* Chicago, IL: University of Chicago Press.

Flook, L., Goldberg. S. B., Pinger, L., & Davidson, R. J. (2015). Promoting prosocial behavior and self-regulatory skills in preschool children through a mindfulness-based kindness curriculum. *Developmental Psychology, 51*(1), 44–51.

Freire, P. (2005/1970). *Pedagogy of the oppressed 30th anniversary edition.* M.B. Ramos (Trans.). New York: Continuum.

Frymier, A.B. (1993). The impact of teacher immediacy on students' motivation: Is it the same for all students? *Communication Quarterly, 41*(4), 454–464.

Garfinkel, S. N., & Critchley, H. D. (2013). Interoception, emotion, and brain: New insights link internal physiology to social behavior. Commentary on "Anterior cortex mediates bodily sensibility and social anxiety" by Teresawa, et. al. (2012). *Social Cognitive Affective Neuroscience, 8*(3), 231–234.

Goleman, D. (2012). *Emotional intelligence: Why it can matter more than IQ.* New York, NY: Bantam.

Greene, J. D. (2004, October). The neural bases of cognitive conflict and control in moral judgement. *Neuron, 44*(2), 389–400.

Greene, J. D. (2009, June). Pushing moral buttons: The interaction between personal force and intention in moral judgment. *Cognition, 11*(13), 364–371.

Greene, J. D. (2014, July). Beyond point and shoot morality: Why cognitive (neuro)science matters. *Ethics, 124*(4), 695–726.

Greene, J. D., Sommerville, R. B., Nystrom, L. E., Darley, J. M. & Cohen, J. D. (2001, September 14). An fMRI investigation of emotional engagement in moral judgment. *Science, 293*(5537), 2105–2108.

Hagstrum, J. H. (1982). *Sex and sensibility: Ideal and erotic love from Milton to Mozart.* Chicago, IL: University of Chicago Press.

Haidt, J., McCanley, C. & Rogers, P. (1994). Individual differences in sensitivity to disgust: A scale sampling seven domains of disgust elicitors. *Personality and Individual Differences, 16*(5), 701–713.

Hamrick, W. S. (2002). *Kindness and the good society: Connections of the heart.* Albany, NY: State University of New York Press.

Hubal, R. C., Kizakevich, P. N., Guinn, C. I., Merino, K. D., & West, S. L. (2000). The virtual standard patient: Simulated patient-practitioner dialogue for patient interview training. *Research Triangle Institute.* Available from https://www.ncbi.nim.nih.gov/pubmed/10977526

Hume, D. (1777/1965). *An enquiry concerning human understanding.* Upper Saddle River, NJ: Prentice Hall.

Jensen, E. (2005). *Teaching with the brain in mind* (2nd ed.). Danvers, MA: Association for Supervision and Curriculum Development.

Johnson, C. (1963). *Old time schools and school books.* New York, NY: Dover.

Johnson, D. W., & Johnson, R. T. (2004). The three C's of promoting social and emotional learning. In J. Zins, R. P. Weissberg, M. C. Wang, & H. J. Walberg, (Eds.), *Building academic success and emotional learning* (pp. 40–58). New York, NY: Teachers College Press.

Jones, L.H. (Ed.). (1903). *The Jones fourth reader.* Boston: Ginn & Company.

Jones, W. T. (1969). *A history of Western philosophy: Hobbes to Hume* (2nd ed.). New York, NY: Harcourt, Brace, & World.

Kant, I. (1785/2013). *The metaphysics of morals.* Cambridge, UK: Cambridge University Press.

Kant, I. (1781/2008). *Critique of pure reason.* M. Weigel (Trans.). London: Penguin Classics.

Knight, J. (2011, October). What good coaches do. *Educational Leadership, 69*(2), 18–22.

Kohlberg, L. (1981). *The philosophy of moral development: Moral stages and the idea of justice.* New York, NY: Harper & Row.

Leagans, J. P. (1964). A concept of needs. *Journal of Cooperative Extension, 11*(89), 89–96.

Ledoux, J. (1996). *The emotional brain.* New York, NY, Simon & Schuster.

Lickona, T. (1991) *Educating for character: How our schools can teach respect and responsibility.* New York, NY: Bantam Books.

Lockwood, A. (1997). *What is character education?* In A. Molnar, (Ed.), *The construction of children's character. 96th yearbook of the national society for the study of education, Part II.*

Maccoby, E. E., & Martin, J. A. (1983). Socialization in the context of the family: Parent-child interaction. In P. H. Mussen, (Ed.), *Handbook of child psychology, Vol. 4.* (pp. 1–101). Hoboken, NJ: Wiley.

MacIntire, A. (1965). *After virtue*. London, UK: Bloomsbury.

Martin, M. W. (1997). Professional distance. *International Journal of Applied Philosophy, 11*(2), 39–50.

Maslow, A. H., Frager, R., & Fadiman, J. (1970). *Motivation and personality, Vol. 2*. New York, NY: Harper and Row.

McClellan, B. E. (1999). *Moral education in America: Schools and the shaping of character from colonial times to the present*. New York, NY: Teachers College Press.

McGuffey, W. H. (1836). *McGuffey's eclectic first reader*. Cincinnati: Truman & Smith.

McGuffey, W. H. (1853). *Mcguffey's newly revised rhetorical guide or fifth reader of the eclectic series*. New York, NY: Clark, Austin, & Smith.

McGuffey, W. H. (1866). *Mcguffey's new fourth eclectic reader: Instructive lessons for the young*. Cincinnati, OH: Wilson, Hinkle.

McGuffey, W. H. (1879a). *Mcguffey's first eclectic reader, revised*. New York, NY: American Book Co.

McGuffey, W. H. (1879b). *Mcguffey's fourth eclectic reader, revised edition*. New York, NY: American Book Co.

McGuffey, W. H. (1881). *Mcguffey's eclectic primer, revised*. New York, NY: American Book Co.

McGuffey, W. H. (1886). *Mcguffey's new fifth eclectic reader: Exercises for schools*. Cincinnati, OH: Sargent, Wilson, & Hinkle.

Mill, J. S. (1859/2002). *On liberty*. New York, NY: Dover.

Noddings, N. (1984). *Caring: A feminine approach to ethics and moral education*. Berkeley, CA: University of California Press.

Noddings, N. (2005). *The challenge to care in schools: An alternative approach to education*. New York, NY: Teachers College Press.

Parsons, S., & Mitchell, P. (2002, June). The potential of virtual reality in social skills training for people with autistic spectrum disorders. *Journal of Intellectual Disability Research, 46*(5), 430–443.

Paxton, J. M., Ungar, L., & Greene, J. D. (2012, January/February). Reflection and reasoning in moral judgment. *Cognitive Science, 36*(1), 163–177.

Pert, C. (1997). *Molecules of emotion.* New York, NY: Scribner's.

Phillips, A., & Taylor, B. (2010). *On kindness.* New York, NY: Penguin.

Piaget, J. (1932/1997). *The moral judgment of the child.* New York, NY: Simon & Schuster.

Porter, E. (1849). *The rhetorical reader, consisting of instruction for regulating the voice with a rhetorical notation.* New York, NY: Newman.

Post, E. L. (1975). *The new Emily Post's etiquette.* New York, NY: Funk & Wagnalls.

Postman, N. (1996). *The end of education.* New York, NY: Vintage Books.

Purpel, D. (1997). The politics of character education. In A. Molnar, (Ed.), *The construction of children's character. 96th yearbook of national society for the study of education, Part II* (pp. 140–153). Chicago, IL: University of Chicago Press.

Random Acts. (n.d.). Available from www.randomacts.org

Rawls, J. (1971). *A theory of justice.* Cambridge, MA: Belknap.

Richmond, V. P. (2002, October). Teacher non-verbal immediacy: Uses and outcomes. In J. L. Chesebro & J. C. McCroskey, (Eds.), *Communication for teachers* (pp. 65-82). Boston, MA: Allyn and Bacon.

Ryan, K. & Bohlin, K. (1999). *Building character in schools: Practical ways to bring moral instruction to life.* San Francisco: Jossey-Bass Inc.

Schonert-Reichel, K. (2017). Social and emotional learning and teachers. *The future of children, 27*(1), 137–155.

Shaffer, D. R. (2005). *Social and personality development* (5th ed.). Belmont, CA: Wadsworth.

Shaffer, D. R., & Kipp, K. (2014). *Developmental psychology* (9th ed.). Belmont CA: Wadsworth.

Smetana, J. G. (2018). Heterogeneity in perceptions of parenting among Arab refugee adolescents in Jordan. *Child Development, 89*(5), 1786–1802.

Smith, A. (1776/1976). *An inquiry into the nature and causes of the wealth of nations.* Chicago, IL: University of Chicago Press.

Smith, T.V. (1926). *The democratic way of life.* Chicago, IL: University of Chicago Press.

SpreadKindness. (n.d.). Available from https://www.spreadkindness.org

Stanford encyclopedia of philosophy. (2013). Stanford, CA: Center for the Study of Language and Information.

Sternberg, R. J. (1998). A balance theory of wisdom. *Review of General Psychology, 2*(4), 347–365.

Stinnet, H. (2018, September 18). *How 1-on-1 time with students made me a better teacher.* Available from https://www.edsurge.com/news/2018-9-18-how-1-on-1-time-with-students-made-me-a-better-teacher

Stroop, J. R. (1935). Studies of interference in serial verbal reactions. *Journal of Experimental Psychology, 18*(6), 643–662.

Sung, K. (2018, June 18). Learning mindfulness centered on kindness to oneself and others. *KQED Mindshift.* Available from https://www.kqed.org/mindshift/51308/learning-mindfulness-centered-on-kindness-to-oneself-and-others

Taylor, R. D., Oberle, E., Durlak, J. A., & Weissberg, R. P. (2017, July/August). Promoting positive youth development through school-based social and emotional learning intervention: A meta-analysis of follow-up effects. *Child Development, 88*(4), 1156–1171.

The royal primer: Or, an easy and pleasant guide to the art of reading. (1787). London, UK: Cornhull, Bolton.

The two Sunday school boys; or the history of Thomas and Joseph. (1832). Philadelphia: American Sunday School Union.

Twain, M. (1870). *The story of the good little boy who did not prosper.* Available from http://twain.lib.virginia.edu/tomsawye/goodboy.html

Tyack, D. (1967). *Turning points in American educational history.* Lexington, MA: Xerox College.

Tyack, D. & Hansot, E. (1982). *Managers of virtue: Public school leadership in America 1820–1980.* New York, NY: Basic Books.

Von Manen, M. (2016). *The tact of teaching: The meaning of pedagogical thoughtfulness.* New York, NY: Routledge.

Walker, A. D. M. (1989). Virtue and character. *Philosophy, 64*(289), 349–362.

Warren, L. (1990). *Sensibility in transformation: Creative resistance to sensibility from the augustans to the romantics: Essays in honor of Jean Hagstrom.* S.M. McMillan Conger (Ed.). Rutherford: Fairleigh Dickenson Press.

Webster, N. (1810). *The American spelling book, containing the rudiments of the english language.* Middletown, Connecticut, William H. Niles.

White, J. B. (1984). *When words lose their meaning: Constitutions and reconstitutions of language, character and community.* Chicago, IL: University of Chicago Press.

Wiggins, D. (2007). A sensible subjectivism. In R. Shafer-Landau & T. Cuneo (Eds.), *Foundations of Ethics* (pp. 145–156). Malden, MA: Blackwell.

Williams, R. (1976). *Keywords: A vocabulary of culture and society.* New York, NY: Oxford University Press.

Wilson, J., Williams, N., & Sugarman, B. (1967). *Introduction to moral education.* New York, NY: Penguin.

Wilson, M. (1881). *Lippincott's fifth reader.* Philadelphia, PA: J.B. Lippincott Co.

Wollstonecraft, M. (2008 /1788). *Mary, a fiction.* London, Dodo Press.

Wright, W. F. (1970). *Sensibility in English prose fiction, 1760–1814: A reinterpretation.* New York, NY: Russell and Russell.

Zins, J., Weissberg, R. P., Wang, M. C., & Walberg, H. J. (Eds.). (2004). *Building academic success and emotional learning: What does the research say?*. New York, NY: Teachers College Press.

Zull, J. E. (2002). *The art of changing the brain: Enriching the practice of teaching by exploring the biology of learning*. Sterling, VA: Stylus.

Steve Broidy was born in 1947 in Oakland, California, but grew up in Columbus, Ohio. His parents were both pharmacists and owned their own pharmacy for many years on that city's north side.

After attending public schools in Columbus, Broidy attended Ohio State University from 1965 to 1969. He graduated with a Bachelor of Arts in English and a Bachelor of Science. in English education. He was a member of OSU's varsity fencing team, and was a two-time Big Ten medalist. He was also a member of Ohio State's College Bowl team that competed on network television.

Broidy taught high school English and creative writing from 1969 to 1972 before going back to OSU for graduate school. He was a teaching assistant during his doctoral work and also served as assistant fencing coach at OSU, where he met his wife Susan who was the captain of OSU's women's varsity fencing team. In 1975, while also working as an assistant professor of education at what is now Missouri State University, he completed his doctorate in philosophy of education, with additional work in both philosophy and linguistics.

Dr. Broidy continued to teach at MSU for 26 years. He became full professor, a department head, and chair of the University's faculty senate. He retired from MSU in 2001 but immediately accepted a position at Wittenberg University in Ohio. He taught at Wittenberg until his retirement in 2017. Broidy is currently emeritus professor of education at both Missouri State University and Wittenberg University. He continues to write scholarly papers and has a new love of poetry. His newest book of poetry is *Earth Inside Them* (2018).

Susan Broidy, Dr Broidy's wife of 43 years, is a sculptor who works primarily in wood and glass. They have two children: Dr. Shayna Fasken, a chiropractor, who lives in Missouri with her husband Kevin and their two children, Solomon and Shoshana; and Benjamin, a wine importer and distributor, who lives in California.